Bonnie & Richard,

It's always a
pleasure working with
you!! Wishing you the best
always.

Best.

# SPECTACULAR HOMES
## of Minnesota

AN EXCLUSIVE SHOWCASE OF MINNESOTA'S FINEST DESIGNERS

Published by

# PANACHE
PANACHE PARTNERS, LLC

13747 Montfort Drive, Suite 100
Dallas, Texas 75240
972.661.9884
Fax 972.661.2743
www.panache.com

Publishers: Brian G. Carabet and John A. Shand
Executive Publisher: Steve Darocy
Associate Publisher: Joanie Fitzgibbons
Editors: Elizabeth Gionta and Lauren Castelli
Designer: Mary Elizabeth Acree

Printed in Malaysia

Distributed by Gibbs Smith, Publisher
800.748.5439

PUBLISHER'S DATA

Spectacular Homes of Minnesota

Library of Congress Control Number:  2006929741

ISBN 13:     978-1-933415-46-8
ISBN 10:     1-933415-46-0

First Printing 2007

10 9 8 7 6 5 4 3 2 1

Previous Page: Beson Kading Interior Design Group
See page 15   Photo by Brian Droege

This Page: Walsh Design Group
See page 163   Photo by John Christenson

# SPECTACULAR HOMES
## of Minnesota

AN EXCLUSIVE SHOWCASE OF MINNESOTA'S FINEST DESIGNERS

4

Mention Minnesota, and images of placid lakes surrounded by coniferous forests come to mind. But Minnesota has much more to offer than the 10,000 lakes for which it is so well known. Indeed, with the gently rolling prairies of the west, the rugged coast of the North Shore and the urban sprawl of the Twin Cities, the "Northern Star" is at once rugged and sophisticated, a characteristic embodied by those blessed to call it home.

With a landscape so magnificent and variegated, it is little wonder that Minnesotans desire the same for their homes. Interiors must not only capture the impressive views but also reflect the natural beauty of the surrounding environment. Designers are thus faced with a substantial challenge, one that those whose work graces the pages that follow overcome with grace and panache. While their styles and philosophies vary, all create interiors that enchant and delight those therein—perfectly complementing the world outdoors.

The award-winning designers featured were selected for their talent, artistry and command of their craft. From luxurious lake houses to contemporary city lofts, these magnificent homes display thoughtful, sophisticated designs that epitomize residents' personalities and stylistic proclivities. Each has evolved from its designer's vast historical and cultural knowledge, strict attention to detail and innate aesthetic sensibility coupled with hard work and a genuine passion for design. The result is, in a word, spectacular.

We invite you to get a glimpse into these magnificent homes and enjoy the work of these skilled artisans. Their exquisite designs truly make Minnesota more beautiful.

*Brian Carabet and John Shand*

Publishers

**DESIGNER** PISA DESIGN, INC., page 147

# TABLE OF CONTENTS

**DESIGNER** CHESTER-HOFFMANN & ASSOCIATES, INC., page 29

**DESIGNER** M|A|PETERSON DESIGNBUILD, INC., page 151

# *Minnesota*

AN EXCLUSIVE SHOWCASE OF MINNESOTA'S FINEST DESIGNERS

# CAROL BELZ

## CAROL BELZ & ASSOCIATES, INC.

Throughout Carol Belz's 36-year career in residential interior design, she has incorporated first and foremost a feeling of comfort while simultaneously intertwining a profound respect for her clients' lifestyles, passions and personalities. It is with this approach that she has built an extremely successful practice.

Graduating with a degree in interior design, Carol then acquired what she considers her master's degree, working for one of the foremost interior designers in Minnesota, Del Stanley. With Stanley as mentor, she learned a great deal about professionalism, ethics and remarkable interior design. In 1980, after working independently in a large design studio, she started her own business with two partners and in 1990, formed Carol Belz & Associates, Inc.

Carol does not strive for a signature aesthetic look. A client once commented that she had been surprised to realize that many of the beautiful homes she had recently visited, none looking like the other, were all created by Carol and her team. Carol had achieved her

goal with those homeowners by conveying an aesthetic interpretation of their lives without letting her own subjective ideas dominate the visual results.

As she has built her clientele, she increasingly enjoys working on second, third and fourth homes all over the country, inspired by new architectural styles and geographical sensibilities. Her projects range from the Maine coast to Seattle, and Cody, Wyoming to the French Quarter in New Orleans. It is during these projects that she gets to spend more time with her clients and immensely enjoys the working relationships that develop. The longevity of the friendships that have formed is the most rewarding part of the design process.

**ABOVE**
Saturated color gives life to a much-used living room showcasing the owner's significant art collection. Family heirlooms contribute to a lively mix of tradition and up-to-date comfort.
*Photograph by Karen Melvin Photography*

**FACING PAGE**
A sophisticated two-story dining area in a river loft integrates traditional and contemporary elements in a graphic, monochromatic interior. Hand-painted photograph by Luis Gonzalez Palma.
*Photograph by Karen Melvin Photography*

As her clients adapt to new stages in their lives, the challenge is to give the newlyweds a beautiful start, the family a kid-friendly environment and the empty nesters a revitalized, exciting look to the future.

"I hope that my clients can look back on their experiences with me as working with a friend, someone who cares deeply about giving them the best possible environment in which to relax, live, entertain and escape the chaotic world outside their doors," Carol said. To her, the personal relationships with clients—both new and old—are as important as the work itself and provide her a diverse platform from which to draw inspiration and energy. Carol helps make dream homes come true, and in return, she enjoys every day working the job of her dreams.

**TOP LEFT**
Sliding walls and a Murphy bed in this loft's master bedroom clear the way for additional entertaining space utilizing the grand piano behind the curtain wall.
*Photograph by Alex Steinberg Photography*

**BOTTOM LEFT**
Living comfortably with a museum-quality collection of contemporary, American Indian, and folk art was key to a young family's approach to interiors and architecture in their new home.
*Photograph by Susan Gilmore Photography*

**FACING PAGE**
A Barry Flanagan bronze overlooks a dining room with 18th-century English Georgian chairs in Fortuny paired with a Rose Tarlow table.
*Photograph by Susan Gilmore Photography*

# MORE ABOUT CAROL ...

**Q&A**

WHAT IS THE MOST FASCINATING HOME YOU'VE BEEN INVOLVED WITH?
A house in the French Quarter because it was so outside of my usual geographical approach to a job.

WHAT DO YOU LIKE MOST ABOUT DOING BUSINESS IN YOUR LOCALE?
The generous spirit and friendliness of the Midwest.

WHAT BOOK ARE YOU READING RIGHT NOW?
*My Life in France* by Julia Child.

DESCRIBE YOUR STYLE PREFERENCES.
My style is timeless, graceful and comfortable in any "look."

CAROL BELZ & ASSOCIATES, INC.
Carol Belz, ASID
275 Market Street, Suite 269
Minneapolis, MN 55405
612.333.1233
Fax 612.333.6006
www.carolbelz.com

# BILLY BESON

## BESON KADING INTERIOR DESIGN GROUP

**D**aring, dynamic and dapper—interior designer Billy Beson is known for his risk-taking style and extraordinary sense of creativity in both his work and life.

"I must admit I do encourage my clients to push the envelope," says Beson, CEO of Beson Kading Interior Design Group. "Big risk, big payoff" is Billy's mantra. He has earned a solid reputation for his ability to envision the space before its completion and his extraordinary ability to convey his concepts to the client. It is the hallmark of Billy's winning formula.

The award-winning designer welcomes projects from the most traditional to extreme high-style Moderne and everything in between. "What keeps me stimulated is the variety of my projects and clientele," says the 25-year veteran of the industry. Having worked across the country—from the Hamptons to Hawaii—each and every project has its own unique character and style, reflecting the clients' needs, wishes and personalities.

Taking ownership of all interior elements, Billy's sense of proportion and scale is the root of his great design. Also not afraid to use color, his interiors are exciting and stimulating, while at the same time nurturing, soothing and empowering.

"I was fortunate to have a wonderful mentor, my uncle, noted Minneapolis interior designer Robert Lenox," Billy says. "He taught me much of what I know, but more importantly, how to celebrate people and have fun doing it."

**ABOVE**
Warm, dramatic and inviting, this large-scale foyer with its Asian influences creates a stunning introduction to this spectacular home. Hand-painted Chinese panels cover hidden doors to china storage and a walk-in coat closet.
*Photograph by Brian Droege*

**FACING PAGE**
Although large in scale, this living room with its warm color palette and sumptuous textures is comfortable and welcoming. The mahogany-paneled ceiling and giant chandelier help to bring the room down to a human scale.
*Photograph by Brian Droege*

BESON KADING INTERIOR DESIGN GROUP
Billy Beson, ASID, IFDA, CID
International Market Square
275 Market Street, Suite 530
Minneapolis, MN 55405
612.338.8187
www.besonkading.com

# RENÉE HALLBERG

## BESON KADING INTERIOR DESIGN GROUP

Classic. Sophisticated. Modern. Interior designer Renée LeJeune Hallberg studied in Europe and was raised with fine arts and antiques. She has taken her refined background and has defined her work to reflect our modern age while still incorporating a classic sense of design and history into her interiors. Whether a Nantucket-style cottage or the Governor's Mansion, Renée has the ability to redefine elegance that is timeless, inviting and most importantly, comfortable.

Renée's niche offers beautiful and practical solutions for her clients. The results are interiors that nurture and support a sense of home and family. "You can have style in your home coupled with sensibility to accommodate an active family," Renée says. A thoughtful listener, she is a natural when it comes to interpreting her clients' needs and desires to create a home with personality—one that appears to have been collected over time. "My clients' homes are about them. Interior design is an opportunity for me to celebrate their special interests and lifestyles." Renée has more than 20 years of experience, and her work has been published regionally and nationally.

**ABOVE**
Captivating and warm, this master bedroom blends European and Asian influences to create a timeless, nurturing retreat.
*Photograph by Lea Babcock*

**FACING PAGE**
The play of the dark, large-scaled dining chairs with the light and airy draperies creates a dramatic result that is fresh, classic and inviting.
*Photograph by Karen Melvin*

BESON KADING INTERIOR DESIGN GROUP
Renée LeJeune Hallberg, Allied Member ASID
International Market Square
275 Market Street, Suite 530
Minneapolis, MN 55405
612.338.8187
www.besonkading.com

# Bruce Kading

## BESON KADING INTERIOR DESIGN GROUP

**B**ruce Kading has received countless recognition by his peers. Bruce is truly an interior designer's designer. With unlimited resources, impeccable style and an uncanny attention to detail, Bruce's interiors are utterly magnificent.

His nationally published projects always show a sense of warmth and a dynamic interplay of texture, depth and color. Bruce's 30-year career is filled with creative environments that definitely stand the test of time.

Bruce, president of Beson Kading Interior Design Group, is known for his strong architectural background—the foundation for his refined interiors that span from Contemporary to Traditional. Using natural fibers, aged woods and beautiful stones, each project is well grounded with an organic feel.

The icing is Bruce's eye for detail. Traveling the world and its diverse markets, the well-heeled designer has selected objects, artwork and little touches that add a sense of age and history to each and every room. Though he brings his touch, Bruce is quick to add, "The most important lesson I've learned is to listen to the clients; they hold the key to a happy home."

**ABOVE**
The antique settee at the foot of the bed in the master suite is reupholstered in bronze cut velvet with nail trim and elegant braid, topped off with luscious fringed down pillows of damask and cut velvet. It provides a nice contrast to the casualness of another antique Bessarabian Kilim.
*Photograph by Brad Daniels*

**FACING PAGE**
The screened porch in this French farmhouse with reclaimed wood floors, stucco walls and a ceiling made of saplings with hand-hewn beams has the feel of an indoor room enhanced by warm colors, textures and an antique Bessarabian Kilim from Romania.
*Photograph by Karen Melvin*

BESON KADING INTERIOR DESIGN GROUP
Bruce Kading, ASID, CID
International Market Square
275 Market Street, Suite 530
Minneapolis, MN 55405
612.338.8187
www.besonkading.com

# SHELLEY CARR
# GARY MANDEL

BAKER COURT INTERIORS

K indred spirits since they met in an eighth-grade art class, Gary Mandel and Shelley Carr share a passion for design that is both raw and rugged while maintaining a simple sense of sophistication. They are a unique team whose strong family values play an important role in how they conduct their business lives. Their clients will tell you that what initially attracted them to work with Gary and Shelley was the way they listened to their visions and dreams. Clients keep coming back because of Gary and Shelley's ability to turn those visions and dreams into reality.

It is not likely that either Gary or Shelley would have been able to foresee that a business partnership would evolve from their junior high school friendship. Gary was committed to developing his artistic talents, which he pursued in college, while Shelley was immediately attracted to the study of interior design. After college, they both embarked on careers in design with each encountering diverse and varied mentors and job experiences. While working together in the same firm, they shared a professional epiphany that there was a niche of potential clients who were looking for the sort of design vision they could provide, and Baker Court Interiors was born.

Baker Court Interiors' founding philosophy is to provide their clients with "Design For Real Life." Grounded by the core values they have each built their lives around, they find the importance

**LEFT**
A stately structure, this St. Croix River home is about quality and comfort. All main-level floors are French Limestone, complemented with walnut cabinets and trim. The kitchen/hearth room carries its own quiet splendor. Wall sconces and chandeliers are circa 1940 Murano glass.
*Photograph by Phillip C. Mueller*

**ABOVE**
The steel-cabled ceiling combined with richly stained cement floors and a unique blend of furniture adorn this large room. Upholstery fabrics range from mohair to silk.
*Photograph by Phillip C. Mueller*

**FACING PAGE TOP**
An envious location, this waterfront home has fluid space and is dominated by curving forms and simple lines. Water cascading down a 13,000-pound basalt water feature adds peaceful comfort.
*Photograph by Phillip C. Mueller*

**FACING PAGE BOTTOM**
Raw materials combined with sophisticated design create a unique master bath. Water-colored glass lines the shower walls, adding a little jewel within the natural environment.
*Photograph by Phillip C. Mueller*

of practicality and good design are of timeless value. This philosophy has matured and grown as the dynamics of their lives have played out. They are both married, and each has two children of similar ages. Gary and Shelley are often able to help a client plan with the entire family in mind, offering pragmatic advice on what the future may hold as each designer proudly passed that grand milestone of having raised their children into adulthood.

Gary and Shelley love the exhilaration that comes from the close relationships they develop with clients. The blending of vision and experience leads to a common search for creating a unique space that radiates warmth and friendship, life and light. Taking a holistic view of each client's life, family and future dreams gives them a perspective to work from. They can create a fusion of color, fabric, materials and finishes that represents a larger legacy rather

than just an isolated place of design. To say they are customer-centric understates their commitment and focus to clients as the heart of their design work.

Clients love working with Gary and Shelley. Their "working studio" integrates clients into the center of the design process. The collaboration that takes place in this special space creates a union of diverse experiences seeking to evolve and embrace the possibilities.

**ABOVE**
A warm gathering place for a large combined family features natural tones with surprising bursts of accent color. Multiple seating areas create great conversation areas. The early 20th-century teak horse, the custom-designed, hand-made, colorful leaf rug and the retro-length draperies all add to the casual personality of the home.
*Photograph by Phillip C. Mueller*

**FACING PAGE**
Clean lines and warm colors mix with the reconstituted wenge wood floors to create an urban feel. Stainless steel counters play with the antique table and chairs.
*Photograph by Phillip C. Mueller*

It is out of this collaboration that homeowners dictate the heart, soul, tradition, spirit and personality of every home that they design. Gary and Shelley are serious about their responsibility to realize clients' design dreams while keeping their focus clear and directed. They are also serious about making sure the process is fun. One cannot help but notice the gleam in their eyes and the smiles on their faces as they share their creative and dramatic ideas and excitement for turning a home into a beloved space of joy and contentment.

Gary and Shelley find that a key element to their success is an appreciation for the integrity and quality of materials. They prefer materials that have been hand-touched—that is, materials whose final shape and design have been achieved through interaction by human hands. The connection of one human to another creates a profound union of beauty and comfort and transforms a home into a sanctuary.

When musing about future goals, they realize their firm is right where they have always wanted to be. They are looking for new ways to incorporate sustainable design features into their work and to find new ways of reinvigorating their creativity. They show no signs of slowing down, which is good news to all who aspire to a design that is real for their lives.

**ABOVE**
Great room of a cottage-inspired lake home. A vaulted, custom-stained tongue-and-groove pine ceiling and character-grade oak floors combined with the warm enhanced woodwork accentuate the carefree lake-home atmosphere.
*Photograph by Tod Buchanan*

**FACING PAGE**
This kitchen has a workable layout combined with a sense of whimsical energy. The dirty-green and dark-blue accent cabinetry has become an artsy, eye-catching addition.
*Photograph by Phillip C. Mueller*

# Q&A

## MORE ABOUT SHELLEY & GARY ...

WHAT IS THE BEST PART OF BEING INTERIOR DESIGNERS?

To realize the connections that we have with our clients, and to make a profound difference in their lives.

YOU CAN TELL WE LIVE IN THIS LOCALE BECAUSE WE ...

Love to use wool materials because of wool's warmth, comfort and durability.

WHAT ONE ELEMENT OF STYLE OR PHILOSOPHY HAVE YOU STUCK WITH FOR YEARS THAT STILL WORKS FOR YOU TODAY?

We always assure our clients: We'll take you to the edge, but we won't let you fall in.

WHAT IS A SINGLE THING YOU DO TO BRING A DULL HOUSE TO LIFE?

Add color to the walls.

BAKER COURT INTERIORS
Shelley Carr
Gary Mandel
821 Raymond Avenue, Suite 160
St. Paul, MN 55114
651.645.7779
Fax 651.645.8852
www.bakercourtinteriors.com

# JEAN
# CHESTER HOFFMANN

## CHESTER-HOFFMANN & ASSOCIATES, INC.

Jean Chester Hoffmann, ASID, of Chester-Hoffmann & Associates, Inc. prides herself on being an extremely versatile interior designer who transcends styles in all facets of design, creating unique and wonderful spaces, no matter how diverse and detailed.

Chester-Hoffmann & Associates, Inc. was founded in 1989; however, Jean created fine interior spaces for almost 20 years prior to establishing this business. Why has her business continually thrived so successfully over all of these years? Jean believes it is because of the philosophy of her mentor, her father. He taught her by his successful example that with sincere determination and hard work anything is attainable. Jean and company work in all venues of design, specializing in higher-end residential and what she calls "executive commercial," which includes such spaces as medical, law and professional offices. Her best achievements range diversely from Traditional to Contemporary. In addition to her local clients' residences, she has created everything from lake homes in the Midwest and ski lodges in Colorado, to luxury homes in California, Arizona and Florida. Jean's signature look is understated elegance tailored with a crisp sophistication.

Always trying to emulate her clients' personalities within their homes, Jean believes that it is her keen sensitivity and use of psychology when reading her clients in tandem with her talent that gives her an edge in attaining a project. She always strives to exceed her clients' expectations. Jean believes that when a project is complete it should reflect her client, but always with her signature of perfection.

Chester-Hoffmann & Associates is a full-service design studio. They can work from the initial planning stages of new homes, pre- or post-construction, or with existing residence renovations, including kitchens and bathrooms. Jean's services range from floor-plan design, space planning, lighting, color selection and furniture selection to completing any project with accessories, art and if the project lends itself, antiques.

**ABOVE**
Hand painting of tulips entwining a French ribbon trellis in a gold glaze accented by shades of greens, burgundy, and blues creates a warm country elegance in the powder room off the kitchen hearth area of this Sunfish Lake residence. Artist: Tricia Farrell.
*Photograph by Alex Steinberg*

**FACING PAGE**
This master bedroom's piéce de résistance is the painting "Ethnic Mother and Baby" by Jane Thompson. The rich Asian influence of the four-poster canopy bed flanking this painting creates an aura of unstated elegance in this Wayzata residence.
*Photograph by Alex Steinberg*

Jean is very approachable, never condescending and respectful of clients' budgets. She feels that this contributes to the fact that her business thrives primarily on word-of-mouth referrals.

Jean's philosophy is that fine design and quality products never age, but trends date a home. Jean keeps abreast of the finest new furnishings introduced into the market, trying to implement and combine them with true classics when designing either Traditional or Contemporary environments. Truly driven to success, Jean always strives to create timeless designs that her clients will enjoy for many years.

Her ultimate goal is to create spaces and render designs that complement, inspire, endure over time and exceed her clients' expectations. Once this is accomplished, Jean feels that her work is fulfilled.

**TOP LEFT**
This great room is a colorful palette rich in jewel tones of eggplant and green against a neutral canvas background. This rich play of colors and textures captures a warm invitation of Old World charm in the 1,600-square-foot area of this Sunfish Lake residence.
*Photograph by Alex Steinberg*

**BOTTOM LEFT**
The warmth of neutral embossed design on textural walls completely envelops the spacious kitchen and dining area of this Cedar Isles residence. The space utters crisp, clean simplicity. Black chairs placed around a glass-top stone pedestal table enhance this simple sophistication. Deep raspberry accents on the chair seats and the fresh table arrangement complete an inviting aura.
*Photograph by Alex Steinberg*

**FACING PAGE LEFT**
The elegant play of neutral grays and black makes this Contemporary St. Paul residence the epitome of understated sophistication.
*Photograph by Alex Steinberg*

**FACING PAGE RIGHT**
The brilliance of color in art and accessories are the jewel that completes the tailored sophistication achieved by the contrasting deep charcoal and white in the spacious open living area of this St. Paul residence.
*Photograph by Alex Steinberg*

# MORE ABOUT JEAN ...

**Q&A**

**WHAT IS THE HIGHEST COMPLIMENT THAT YOU HAVE RECEIVED PROFESSIONALLY?**

That I have impeccable taste, an amazingly keen sense of color and an extremely tenacious spirit.

**WHAT SINGLE THING WOULD YOU DO TO BRING A DULL HOUSE TO LIFE?**

Design with a simple neutral scheme and then accessorize with color.

**WHAT IS THE MOST IMPORTANT PART OF THE DESIGN PROCESS?**

I'm a perfectionist! Every facet of any design project is of equal importance in achieving the best results.

**WHAT IS THE BEST PART OF BEING AN INTERIOR DESIGNER?**

Constantly being introduced to new products is exciting; it's like a gift. There is always something new in the design field. Equally important, I am blessed with wonderful clients who give me the opportunity to incorporate an amazing spread of resources, using my creativity when designing their residences.

**CHESTER-HOFFMANN & ASSOCIATES, INC.**
Jean Chester Hoffmann, ASID
3948 West 50th Street, Suite 204
Edina, MN 55424
952.925.9871
Fax 952.925.9872

# KERRY
# CIARDELLI-OLSON
## VICTORY

**K**erry Ciardelli-Olson is a firm believer in the philosophy that a home should not only be seen but enjoyed, as well. While relatively new to the interior design business, Kerry long nurtured an acute sensitivity toward that which is beautiful, elegant and vintage. Growing up with a mother who lived by the tenet that quality, not quantity, is paramount in home design, Kerry learned very early to appreciate fine furnishings and accessories. An antique dealer by trade, Kerry's mother instilled in her a love of home décor—a background that impelled Kerry to pursue her current career and continues to permeate her daily life.

Kerry's decision to turn her love of interiors into a profession was largely inspired by her work renovating homes to put back on the market. Her knowledge of antiques coupled with her frequent travels around the globe gave her insight into a variety of available furnishings and techniques, and her work was thus very well received by potential home buyers. Recognizing that her talent was a potentially lucrative pursuit, she decided to open

a home store in which to share the treasures she found in her travels. She visited a variety of flea markets in London, Paris and Florence, where she made strong contacts and obtained a broad education about unique and highly coveted items for the home. When the doors to Victory opened in 2003, Kerry officially began to offer her finds and her expertise to Minneapolis residents.

Three years later, Victory is a vibrant addition to the community. Offering luxurious and rare items such as English silver servers and utensils, antique cake stands, etched-glass pieces and fine French linens, the shop also features exclusive designer pieces from the likes of

**ABOVE**
An antique gilded, carved-wood marble-topped console from Victory sits atop a checkerboard marble floor in this welcoming entry to the designer's home.
*Photograph by Kim Cornelison*

**FACING PAGE**
Soft silk curtains frame the large windows in this bright, warm living room. The blue 1930's chair was completely reinvented by the designer while the washable white damask sofa holds 18th-century tapestry pillows, beautifully blending past and present.
*Photograph by Kim Cornelison*

Christopher Spitzmiller and Anna Weatherly. The shop is unique in that it also serves as Kerry's design office, from which she takes on a select few residential projects for Victory patrons. Her interior design work often involves additions to homes—a carriage house above a garage, perhaps—room renovations and even small-scale projects such as accessorizing a bedroom or bath. With the items in the store at her fingertips, she can offer her clients both her professional eye and the variety of products and contacts Victory affords.

While Kerry maintains that people should surround themselves with those things they find beautiful, she also insists upon function and comfort in a home. One's house should not serve as a museum in which to display untouchable items but instead should support the

**ABOVE LEFT**
A 19th-century Venetian mirror and vintage crystal pieces twinkle in the dining room corner. A hot pink velvet ottoman beneath the bar tray holds a Kevin O'Brien pillow and adds a bold burst of color.
*Photograph by Kim Cornelison*

**ABOVE RIGHT**
The plush sofa encourages diners to cozy up to the farm-style table set with heirloom china and lends a unique and comfortable feel to the designer's kitchen. The green-and-white curtains and sofa pillows are a bright, welcoming touch.
*Photograph by Kim Cornelison*

**FACING PAGE**
The blue Christopher Spitzmiller lamp provides a unique light source and pops against the silver-sage walls in this formal dining room. A flea-market portrait hangs above an antique chair, refinished and recovered by the designer in white duck cloth.
*Photograph by Kim Cornelison*

habits and mirror the lifestyles of those who live within. Kerry therefore urges people to pull their heirlooms out of the attic and incorporate them into their living spaces, thus giving these prized items the attention and prominence they deserve. Believing that children and pets are the heart of a household she suggests that families choose hardy, washable fabrics for upholstery, further encouraging people to bring sofas and other comfortable seating into their kitchens where the most time is spent and place televisions in living rooms to foster gatherings therein. Kerry thus designs homes in which every room is used, and those used more frequently promote the utmost sense of solace and pleasure.

Kerry's exquisite designs have been featured in *Better Homes & Gardens, Mpls. St. Paul Magazine* and the *Star Tribune*. She persists in her search for unique pieces by traveling broadly and attends numerous home and gift shows, broadening her network of vendors

and craftspeople, alike. While her own home reflects her feminine, sophisticated taste, she emphasizes the client's personal style in each residence she designs. Between its numerous wares and Kerry, herself, Victory truly houses inestimable gifts.

**ABOVE**
Entirely gutted and refurbished by the designer to preserve the architectural integrity of her 1920's home, this traditional kitchen features shuttered windows, old-fashioned cupboards and a farmhouse sink along with the weighty, double-bullnosed Carrera marble-topped island.
*Photograph by Kim Cornelison*

**FACING PAGE LEFT**
The view through the dining room into the living room features Barbara Barry chairs, a 1920's chandelier and a late-century, hand-painted and gilded Italian armoire.
*Photograph by Kim Cornelison*

**FACING PAGE RIGHT**
Enameled dove-white mouldings create a dramatic contrast to the dark-stained wood of the entry's floor and staircase. Etchings of Notre Dame done by a 12-year-old child adorn the walls, and silk curtains frame the landing's large window.
*Photograph by Kim Cornelison*

# MORE ABOUT KERRY...

## MY FRIENDS WOULD TELL YOU THAT...

I love spending time in my home with my daughter, my friends and my dogs. A home is a refuge, and in mine, I cultivate a celebratory atmosphere on a daily basis. Every night, the candles are lit and the music is playing!

## WHAT'S THE BEST PART ABOUT BEING A SHOP OWNER AND DESIGNER?

Gathering people together for good food, good music, great conversation and lots of laughter. I believe that comfortable spaces help create togetherness, so all my rooms—and the events I hold at my store—are beautiful, comfortable and welcoming.

## WHAT IS THE ONE DESIGN PHILOSOPHY YOU RECOMMEND TO ALL HOMEOWNERS?

Surround yourself with beauty, things you truly love and enjoy. Unique treasures always help me get through life's more pedestrian tasks. Paying my bills is always easier while sipping coffee from a beautiful cup I uncovered at an English flea market.

VICTORY
Kerry Ciardelli-Olson
3505 West 44th Street
Minneapolis, MN 55410
612.926.8200
Fax 612.926.8777
www.shopvictory.com

# SHELLY RIEHL DÀVID

## RIEHL DESIGNS, INC.

If one were to sum up Shelly Riehl Dàvid's style in one word, it would be *fun*. With nearly 20 years in the business, Shelly knows how to cultivate a sense of adventure in every project she and her team at Riehl Designs undertakes. Shelly's fearless use of bold, vibrant colors and eclectic design accents and accessories sets her apart from regional designers and adds to her designs' global appeal.

Indeed, her clientele spans the globe. While Minnesota-based, Shelly has designed primary residences, turnkey vacation homes and businesses across the country and in exotic locales. Her knowledge of and access to international sources of such elements as Fortuny lighting, hand-blown Murano glass and custom-made Milanese furniture are of great value to those wishing to achieve unique home designs.

*Unique* is no overstatement. Shelly insists that her design is constantly evolving, so much so that she never creates the same look twice. Her extraordinary interiors have earned her recognition in such publications as *Florida Design, Miami Home & Décor, European Homes & Gardens, Florida Travel & Life, Decorating Spaces* and Britain's *Escape to ...*

*Florida*. Shelly recently won the opportunity to complete a Palm Beach home for HGTV's "Designers' Challenge." Truly, Riehl Designs offers one-of-a-kind design experiences that appeal to all.

**ABOVE**
This intriguing room features exotic details as depicted in the ostrich-embossed leather sofa, zebra rug, Moroccan lighting and custom linen draperies on hand-forged iron rods.
*Photograph by Greg Page*

**FACING PAGE**
This elegant room features dramatic draperies, a Fortuny chandelier and Murano glass lighting, along with custom furniture from Milan.
*Photograph by Greg Page*

RIEHL DESIGNS, INC.
Shelly Riehl Dàvid, IFDA
7929 Victoria Drive
Victoria, MN 55386
952.440.4175
Fax 866.229.9761
www.riehldesigns.com

# BETTY DUFF
## DESIGN INNOVATIONS

Betty Duff of Design Innovations creates a very classic design with a graceful casual elegance that her clients find simply fabulous. With the help of her two design associates, Pepper Eggers and Annie Noel, Betty controls everything comprehensively, from the designs to the installations of projects. She strives for the best and accepts nothing less for her clients, whom she calls friends because of the special relationship that they develop over the course of a project.

Originally from Tyler, Texas, as a teenager Betty started designing window displays for her mother's store and the Pier 1 Imports next door. She graduated from the University of Texas at Austin in 1975 with a degree in interior design and moved to Minnesota in 1983, where she would open her interior design business in 1987. Since then she has steadily amassed a large and dedicated clientele base with her wonderful designs.

One of the greatest aspects of Betty's success is customer service. She returns every call that she receives. She has gotten some rather large projects from answering cold phone calls from her future clients. This dedication to customer service has provided a generous living for the blessed interior designer, and when speaking with students interested in interior design, she always stresses this key to success.

In the Midwest, homeowners are looking for living environments where they can entertain and raise a family, which is why Betty loves to work in Minnesota and the surrounding areas. "There is truly a value to what they are purchasing and putting in their homes," Betty said.

When designing a space for a client, Betty always tries to include an "artistic flair." Usually, it is a hand painting or some other artisan handiwork. A very detailed-oriented designer, she tries to have a hands-on approach to her projects, especially when it comes to choosing hardware, stonework, cabinet details and anything involved, from "A to Z."

Betty says that function always comes first, and the "frou-frou" comes second. She believes a room has to function first before it can become a successful design, and the "fluff" is what you add to it to make it more dynamic. In the future, Betty will continue working with existing clients and keep building upon those cherished relationships.

**ABOVE**
Utilizing an heirloom buffet, this formal powder room of a Medina family is highlighted by a custom-designed glass art vessel for the countertop, with upholstered walls adding to the space.
*Photograph by Alex Steinberg*

**FACING PAGE**
Influenced by three years of living in Europe, Rich and Michelle Meyer of Chanhassen wanted to showcase their collections in this lovely entertainment room.
*Photograph by Alex Steinberg*

**TOP LEFT**
Diane and Mark Cary of Edina always dreamed of an entertaining space adjacent to their pool. Utilizing imported bamboo for the ceiling and stone materials throughout, the room now has an outdoor atmosphere.
*Photograph by Alex Steinberg*

**BOTTOM LEFT**
The McCary's formal living room features stone pillars highlighted by an Old World chandelier. A balance of textured walls, fabrics, sheer panels, eclectic art and lighting brings enjoyment to their guests.
*Photograph by Alex Steinberg*

**FACING PAGE LEFT**
In this grand living room are dark, rich colors of eggplant with pewter accents accompanied by the formal fireplace, which brings focus to the multiple seating areas.
*Photograph by Alex Steinberg*

**FACING PAGE RIGHT**
In the formal rotunda entry of a Medina family home, guests are greeted by the wonderful usage of a colorful textured wall tapestry with an unusual granite stone underfoot.
*Photograph by Alex Steinberg*

# MORE ABOUT BETTY ...

NAME ONE THING MOST PEOPLE DON'T KNOW ABOUT YOU.

I graduated from the University of Texas at Austin in 1975 with a Bachelor of Science in interior design.

WHAT DO YOU LIKE MOST ABOUT WORKING IN YOUR LOCALE?

In the Twin Cities there is truly a Midwestern eclectic mixture of things. There is truly a value to what clients are purchasing and putting in their homes. They are looking for homes in which their kids can grow up and they can entertain.

WHAT ONE TECHNIQUE HAVE YOU USED FOR YEARS THAT STILL WORKS FOR YOU TODAY?

Whenever my clients work with me, they tell me that I'm detail oriented in terms of hardware, stonework and cabinetry and that I am involved in the project from A to Z.

DESIGN INNOVATIONS
Betty Duff, owner
6521 McCauley Trail West
Edina, MN 55439
952.903.5152
Fax 952.903.5153

# MICHELE BOUCHER EICH

## EICH INTERIOR DESIGN

**W**hen Michele Eich was a little girl, her father was forever stubbing his toe in the middle of the night. That's because his daughter frequently rearranged the furniture in their house. Her poor dad would come home and find his favorite chair—and the rest of the living room furnishings—in what had been, earlier in the day, the dining room and the dining room table where the family TV had been. He may not have minded, but his toes sure did.

Today, Michele still rearranges furniture, though to less detrimental effect. The 33-year-old interior designer operates her own full-service residential and commercial design firm and retail home décor store in downtown Minneapolis, giving clients spaces that perfectly suit their needs and delight their hearts.

The Minnesota native and graduate of the University of Minnesota calls her style eclectic. She likes to blend Traditional and Contemporary, mix clean lines with curves and create spaces that are uplifting, clever and unpredictable. And though each client has his or her own design preferences, Michele's goal is always the same: To give that client something they fall in love with, something they crave when they are away from it, something they can come home to and lose themselves in.

A self-described workaholic, Michele is an energetic, down-to-earth person. She has a friendly, light-hearted manner and a natural way of putting others at ease. Those traits are the means to a good end result, as she strives to guide clients out of their safe zones and give them homes that are beyond anything they ever

**LEFT**
Dining/living room, 2006 ASID Showcase Home, Lake Minnetonka, Wayzata, Minnesota.
*Photograph by Karen Melvin*

45

imagined for themselves. "First," she says, "people have to trust you; you have to create an environment where they can be vulnerable."

Clients who have seen her work, whether at a friend's home or a showcase house, know the magic Michele can do. Those who haven't can get a glimpse at her retail shop, which is stocked with furniture and accessories hand-picked by the designer. She travels to markets all over the country, in search of the unexpected. Armoires and bookcases, unusual vases and accent pieces, artwork and area rugs fill the 2,500-square-foot space.

With goods on hand, Michele feels the store gives her a bit of an edge. "Having ready access to interesting things is a shortcut to having to go out and search for them," she says. That's not to say, however, that when a room calls for something truly special she doesn't have, she won't comb the earth for it. There's very little the award-winning designer wouldn't do to give someone a spectacular home.

**TOP LEFT**
Master bedroom, 2003 ASID Showcase Home, Minneapolis, Minnesota.
*Photograph by Elisabeth Groh*

**BOTTOM LEFT**
Kellogg mansion back-entry powder room, 2004 ASID Showcase Home, St. Paul, Minnesota.
*Photograph by Elisabeth Groh*

**FACING PAGE TOP**
Family/dining room, 2006 ASID Showcase Home, Wayzata, Minnesota.
*Photograph by Karen Melvin*

**FACING PAGE BOTTOM**
Kitchen, 2006 ASID Showcase Home, Wayzata, Minnesota.
*Photograph by Karen Melvin*

**TOP LEFT**
Master suite, 2005 ASID Showcase Home, Minneapolis, Minnesota.
*Photograph by Karen Melvin*

**BOTTOM LEFT**
Master suite sitting area, 2005 ASID Showcase Home, Minneapolis, Minnesota.
*Photograph by Karen Melvin*

**FACING PAGE TOP**
Master suite, 2003 ASID Showcase Home, Minneapolis, Minnesota.
*Photograph by Elisabeth Groh*

**FACING PAGE BOTTOM**
Master bath, 2005 ASID Showcase Home, Minneapolis, Minnesota.
*Photograph by Karen Melvin*

# MORE ABOUT MICHELE ...

## Q&A

**WHAT IS SOMETHING MOST PEOPLE DON'T KNOW ABOUT YOU?**

Many are surprised to discover that I love NASCAR. In fact, I used to race cars myself. Were I not a designer, perhaps I would be a race car driver. I dream of one day taking the checkered flag in a car sponsored by Victoria's Secret.

**WHAT SINGLE THING WOULD YOU DO TO BRING A DULL HOUSE TO LIFE?**

Spice up the furnishings. How a space is furnished has the biggest impact. Add an interesting new piece, adjust the traffic pattern, add artwork and textiles—the right elements make a space feel warm.

**WHAT PERSONAL INDULGENCE DO YOU SPEND THE MOST MONEY ON?**

I like to travel. I also like to invest in significant furnishings for my own home. I recently purchased a baby grand piano.

**AWARDS AND RECOGNITION ...**

We earned the People's Choice award for our designs on the 2005 ASID Showcase Home master suite and the 2006 ASID Showcase Home kitchen, dining, living and powder rooms. We've also received accolades for our historic restoration efforts and window treatments, and my designs have been featured in magazines such as *Window Fashions, Midwest Home & Garden, Mpls. St. Paul, Better Homes and Gardens* and on the front cover of the Minneapolis *Star Tribune's*, "Home & Garden" section.

EICH INTERIOR DESIGN
Michele Boucher Eich
Allied Member ASID
21 North East 5th Street
Minneapolis, MN 55403
612.331.1573
www.eichinteriordesign.com

# LINDA ENGLER
# TALLA SKOGMO

## ENGLER SKOGMO INTERIOR DESIGN

The art of living has a lot of fingerprints on it, and no one knows this better than Linda Engler and Talla Skogmo, cofounders of Engler Skogmo Interior Design.

Primarily a residential interior design firm, Engler Skogmo enjoys a nice combination of special commercial projects as well. The firm's bread and butter is magnificent, custom high-end homes.

Linda and Talla were both educated at the University of Minnesota and became acquainted while working at competing firms. Forming a mutual admiration both personally and professionally, they decided to mesh their talents, energy and experience in 2004 with the founding of Engler Skogmo Interior Design.

The designers at Engler Skogmo maintain separate clientele, but are always available to bounce ideas back and forth and act as a sounding board, view a project with "fresh eyes" and suggest a new idea or lend an objective opinion. Though the firm's designers may have different aesthetic approaches to designing an interior, the common threads that run through each project are classic, timeless, clean and well-edited designs.

Avoiding the cookie-cutter designer stereotype, their interiors never have an "Engler Skogmo" signature look to them. They rely on their clients' personalities and lifestyles to dictate the look of each project, focusing on each client's comfort and enjoyment. The designers at Engler Skogmo celebrate, balance and complement each other's strengths which results in dynamic and thoughtful results for the firm's clients.

**ABOVE**
Organic forms and materials merge with the urban skyline in this city-loft gathering space. Graceful, modestly proportioned furniture offers soft curves and classic style.
*Photograph by Greg Page, Page Studios*

**FACING PAGE**
Centrally located, this dining area serves as the heart of the house in an approachable, unpretentious fashion, using the relaxed ambiance of warm wood tones, slate and rustic beams.
*Photograph by Greg Page, Page Studios*

The symbiotic collaboration of client, craftsmen, architects and builders is what excites Linda and Talla about each new project. They share the belief that good design is the result of a process—a process combining talent, skill, experience and most importantly, shared ideas. Above all, a team-oriented environment is stressed, and making the client part of that team is key. It is not just about that particular designer's style; it is about getting their clients' fingerprints on the project as well.

"They don't come to us to get a look," Talla says. "They come to us to help put a collection together, whether the collection involves their children's photos, wonderful pottery from Peru, beautiful rugs or paintings. Clients come to us to help them assemble their lives and take it to the next level."

**TOP LEFT**
The palette of this master bedroom is calming, where rustic alder millwork and beams keep company with elegant textiles and case pieces inclined toward formality—all in comfortable balance.
*Photograph by Greg Page, Page Studios*

**BOTTOM LEFT**
An Asian-inspired screen and grand piano veil the kitchen from the dining area in this urban loft.
*Photograph by Greg Page, Page Studios*

**FACING PAGE LEFT**
Dark wood-frame dining chairs paired with a mid-century chrome-and-glass dining table adds interest and sophistication to this award-winning loft space.
*Photograph by Greg Page, Page Studios*

**FACING PAGE RIGHT**
Pillows in silk and flat-weave cotton rest atop plush mohair upholstery, creating both textural and visual interest.
*Photograph by Greg Page, Page Studios*

# MORE ABOUT LINDA & TALLA ...

WHO HAS HAD THE BIGGEST INFLUENCE ON YOUR CAREERS?

Our mothers.

WHAT ONE PHILOSOPHY HAVE YOU STUCK WITH FOR YEARS THAT STILL WORKS FOR YOU TODAY?

Less is more.

IF YOU COULD ELIMINATE ONE DESIGN TECHNIQUE FROM THE WORLD, WHAT WOULD IT BE?

Faux finishing ... faux anything!

ENGLER SKOGMO INTERIOR DESIGN
Linda Engler, ASID
Talla Skogmo, ASID
5100 Edina Industrial Boulevard, Suite 200
Edina, MN 55439
952.746.2007
Fax 952.746.2008
www.englerskogmo.com

# TIMOTHY FLEMING

## TIMOTHY G. FLEMING, INC.

Timothy Fleming is not only a designer of interiors, he is a connoisseur of fine craftsmanship as well. While his formal education is in the fine arts, he began working for designer William Nakashian at age 20 and thus had the good fortune to be exposed at an early age to high-end homes, intelligent and affluent clientele and first-rate craftspeople. His experiences fed his fascination with design and helped launch what has proven to be a successful 30-year career in the field.

With his solo-run firm, Timothy G. Fleming, Inc., which he opened 11 years ago and now operates out of St. Paul, he designs residential interiors not only in Minnesota but also in such diverse locales as Hawaii, Aspen, Sanibel Island and Chicago. Indeed, he does 50 percent of his work outside his home state, and he travels extensively throughout Europe to seek out ideas and sources of design elements. Timothy shares his vast compendium of resources, offering a broad selection of unique and interesting furniture pieces, textiles, antiques and other items to which clients would not be exposed otherwise.

The caliber of his primary influences speaks to Timothy's discerning sensibility. Timothy credits famous designer Jed Johnson and renowned collector Dr. Albert Barnes for his keen ability to successfully mix styles within a room to achieve aesthetically sound results. Like those two innovators before him, Timothy designs with the mindset that a variety of contrasting and complementary pieces carefully combined can yield the least predictable, most visually interesting results: "I juxtapose colors, lines, textures and cultures in such a way that while the overall effect might test one's sense of order, it also engages one's imagination and develops one's aesthetic awareness."

**ABOVE**
The French commode circa 1780 is juxtaposed with a Deco Schneider vase/lamp circa 1930 and a Joseph Haske painting circa 2003.
*Photograph by Alex Steinberg*

**FACING PAGE**
Glazing the Tudor oak woodwork in taupe/cream created a bright, stimulating background for the traditional Persian, Viennese, English and American furnishings.
*Photograph by Karen Melvin*

Timothy's knack for creating working anachronisms stems from the high value he places on the integrity of each piece. He respects the authenticity of every element of a design, insisting upon stylistic accuracy in reproductions and educating clients as to their historical contexts and origins. Taking a cue from one of his mentors, famous textile designer Jack Lenor Larsen, Timothy underscores the collaborative process that goes into every aspect of a project, from those who grow the materials that comprise the various items used to those who install them into a home. While he shares his vast knowledge and often

**ABOVE**
18th-century Venetian and French furniture "bookend" the bronze branch mirror circa 2004 by Van der Straeten.  The new Regency caned bergeres flank the period Regency center table circa 1890.
*Photograph by Alex Steinberg*

**RIGHT**
A starburst crystal fixture circa 1970 hovers over woven copper curtains which enhance the Russian rug circa 1890 and the Biedermeier bench circa 1840.
*Photograph by Alex Steinberg*

**FACING PAGE**
The Savonnerie carpet inspired the custom steel bed, which reflects the silvered/mirrored Italian wall sconces circa 1790 and the highlights in the wall finish.
*Photograph by Alex Steinberg*

brutally honest opinion with all of his clients, he insists upon honoring their wishes and gives them full stylistic control.

Every opportunity is taken to expand and enrich his knowledge. He has actively involved himself in every stage of the design process, deepening his passion for craft by studying artisans at work. Indeed, he approaches those craftspeople whose creations he admires and asks to join them to learn about the processes and materials that go into producing their beautiful works of art.

Timothy's proactive approach to his design education stems from his view that the world is in essence his classroom. Old and new art, music, film and fashion, nature and even food inspire and provoke his creativity and influence the renovations, additions and new projects he undertakes. A self-proclaimed amoeba, Timothy soaks up the culture that surrounds

him and refines and distills it to achieve beautiful, sophisticated results. "My hope," he says, "is that after visiting a home I designed, people will leave with the sense that they did not merely view the installation but experienced it in such a way that it will long remain in their memories."

**ABOVE**
Iridescent, pearlized finishes on the walls, ceramic vases, art glass, paintings and botanical fabrics were unexpected in this 1870 mansion.
*Photograph by Elisabeth Groh*

**FACING PAGE LEFT**
This Neoclassical powder room is clad in tertiary colors of the same marble.  The 19th-century French mirror and silver wall sconces complete the style.
*Photograph by Alex Steinberg*

**FACING PAGE RIGHT**
Painted and gilded Swiss dining chairs circa 1780 surround the Baccarat crystal chandelier circa 1890, all framed by the 20th-century silk damask curtains on steel rods.
*Photograph by Alex Steinberg*

# MORE ABOUT TIMOTHY ...

## Q&A

WHO ARE YOUR TOP FIVE ROLE MODELS?

William Nakashian, my first mentor, changed my life forever. He opened my eyes to a whole new world of styles, artifacts and decorative objects. He also opened the doors to many of the major leaders in the design industry. I was very lucky.

Jed Johnson repeatedly demonstrated to me the importance of mixing styles with a fresh approach. He was, in my opinion, one of the most important interior designers of the 20th century.

Dr. Albert Barnes taught me the importance of maintaining discipline when juxtaposing design influences. His personal art collection is one of the most incredible in the country. I was fortunate to see it in the museum he created to house it and exhibited exactly as he stipulated—what a treasure!

Jack Lenor Larsen reminds me constantly of the importance of craft. Each and every ingredient of design is invaluable. His passion for life is absolutely addictive. Brainstorming with Jack about design is priceless.

Siah Armajani, international artist, taught me the importance of simplicity. Good, clean design requires nothing more. His gracious, humble demeanor enhances my respect. I am honored and awed by the experience of working on his home.

WHAT DESIGN PHILOSOPHY HAVE YOU STUCK WITH FOR YEARS THAT STILL WORKS FOR YOU TODAY?

I have tried always to be in tune with modernity while maintaining a sensitivity to and respect for tradition.

TIMOTHY G. FLEMING, INC.
Timothy Fleming, ASID
23 South Saint Albans Street
St. Paul, MN 55105
651.291.7310
Fax 651.291.7300

# MAGGIE FLOWERS

## MAGGIE FLOWERS INTERIOR DESIGN

Maggie Flowers will be the first to tell you she never takes interiors literally. Seriously? Yes. Literally? No.

Instead, the Duluth, Minnesota designer approaches her projects with an artistic perspective that is uniquely founded on a rock-solid knowledge of construction and architecture. This knowledge comes from years of education and firsthand experience observing and listening to contractors, builders, electricians and any other tradespeople on the project. No matter what, she's there—working with them—whether they're installing plumbing, drapes, wiring or carpet to ensure that the details are addressed as she and her clients desire.

*Desire* is the key word here. Maggie has an almost overwhelming passion for serenity of space, for comfort, for beauty as spectacular as the Lake Superior setting which frames many of her projects.

Capturing this view, this environment, and translating its scale and color into interior spaces is, in fact, one of Maggie's most exceptional talents. It is no small task, and it requires thoughtful insight and honest, open communication with the client. As a result, Maggie's interiors are clean, never cluttered, never cliché—a natural composition unfolding with organic looseness.

Maggie's firm works primarily on residential projects—from new construction and remodels to historic preservation of stately turn-of-the-century homes that dot Duluth's steep hillside.

**ABOVE**
Goin' Fishin? Dedicated to the man who loves the outdoors, this study features custom cherry cabinetry with leather panels and desk with a carved frieze. The reclaimed hickory floor holds the antique Oushak rug.
*Photograph by Stuart Lorenz*

**FACING PAGE**
Volume speaks: Intimate elegance, comfort and scale are unified with a custom-made floral bordered carpet. Natural stone and a bleached ceiling provide a balance among tall white pine.
*Photograph by Stuart Lorenz*

Incidentally, Maggie Flowers Interior Design is housed in a 100-year-old building, which she painstakingly restored and for which she was honored with a historic preservation award.

Even with such architectural gems all around her, Maggie especially enjoys new construction. Being involved at the architectural stage affords her the opportunity to infuse details from the larger structure into elements such as cabinets or furnishings. For her clients, it brings everything together and creates that vital sense of balance and flow.

Clients may not always be able to verbalize or even understand the importance of that flow, but Maggie's four-person team is adept at guiding and inspiring customers, as well as exposing them to diverse genres of design. That and a 3,000-square-foot showroom filled with accessories and furniture allow clients to easily see what they do and do not want.

For Maggie, this is what design is all about—not fussiness or fanciness, but vision. And her job is to help clients find exactly what they're looking for.

**TOP LEFT**
Natural stone and custom maple cabinetry comprise the organic theme that connects the family room with other spaces. Tall columns in the dining room beyond support the views.
*Photograph by Stuart Lorenz*

**BOTTOM LEFT**
Balance, serenity and harmony subdue the vastness of Lake Superior. Custom cherry cabinetry holds many stories of family and travel.
*Photograph by Jeff Frey*

**FACING PAGE**
Unexpected personality greets a guest to the powder room. Warmth is achieved with color, texture and lighting.
*Photograph by Jeff Frey*

# MORE ABOUT MAGGIE ...

**Q&A**

### WHAT IS ONE RULE YOU ALWAYS FOLLOW?

Things have to make sense. You need to follow a thematic thread that runs through and connects all of your spaces. You establish a presence or "look" as soon as you drive up to a home—the architecture, the site, the exterior coloration—this is what tells you how to approach the inside of a house. Simply put, your entire theme is established at the curb.

### WHAT IS THE BEST PART OF THE PROCESS?

Getting to know my clients and their expectations. Then later, the installation when everyone is wildly excited.

### DO YOU HAVE A SIGNATURE LOOK?

Yes. People can tell my work from other projects mainly because I like deeper, richer colors; I don't do cliché coloring either. I like coming up with new color juxtapositions. And I don't do anything without first analyzing the scale of the elements in the design.

### WHAT HAS BEEN YOUR BIGGEST INFLUENCE?

At the risk of being immodest, I would say that I am self-directed. I have been blessed with an enormous amount of energy, and I have always believed in my own talent.

### WHAT IS YOUR PHILOSOPHY?

Comfort and beauty are not separate entities. It is that simple. Beyond that, we believe integrated design elements have a relationship with the architecture, and that they are not merely superficial applications. That is why we don't just sell the elements, we sell the unique point of view.

### WHAT IS A SINGLE THING YOU WOULD DO TO BRING A DULL HOUSE TO LIFE?

Infuse it with color and light.

**MAGGIE FLOWERS INTERIOR DESIGN**
Maggie Flowers
1434 East Superior Street
Duluth, MN 55805
218.724.8821
Fax 218.724.1170

# R. THOMAS GUNKELMAN
# ANDREW FLESHER

## GUNKELMANFLESHER INTERIOR DESIGN

For more than 40 years, Tom Gunkelman of GunkelmanFlesher Interior Design has been a highly respected design leader in Minnesota and throughout the country. Tom, his business partner Andrew Flesher, and their team of award-winning designers have built an exceptional reputation for innovatively reflecting their clients' interior design dreams, desires and unique sensibilities.

Believing that good design is timeless in both function and nature, Tom, Andrew and their team work in design styles that range from Traditional to Contemporary—often beautifully integrating the two. In fact, Tom's designs tend to be more minimalist, following the words of Mies Van der Rohe's philosophy "less is more."

Projects to GunkelmanFlesher's credit range from lavish lake homes in Minnesota to New York lofts and even a winery in Napa Valley. Among a number of celebrity home projects, they are working on author and humorist Garrison Keillor's New York home.

Andrew, who almost rivals Tom for the number of national "Top Designer" designations, is the perfect design counterbalance. Billed by one magazine as "The Intuitionist," he brings a decidedly different-but-complementary design sense to GunkelmanFlesher's leadership team. Together with their national-award-winning design team, GunkelmanFlesher is a long-established interior design leader that continues to renew itself daily.

**ABOVE**
The lobby of a condominium designed by Andrew Flesher. Features include a restful waterfall, a living room for gathering and a large commercial kitchen.
*Photograph by Alex Steinberg*

**FACING PAGE**
A Minneapolis loft designed by Tom Gunkelman shows the use of timeless, classic furnishings in a utilitarian space.
*Photograph by John Umberger*

GUNKELMANFLESHER INTERIOR DESIGN
R. Thomas Gunkelman
Andrew Flesher
81 South 9th Street, Suite 340
Minneapolis, MN 55402
612.333.0526
Fax 612.333.0528
www.gunkelmanflesher.com

# BRANDI HAGEN
## EMINENT INTERIOR DESIGN, LTD.

For Brandi Hagen, principal of Eminent Interior Design, Ltd., the chemistry of good design, inherent talent and client interaction has been the formula for her firm's continued success. Capturing the vision from inside each of their clients, Brandi Hagen and her team create design solutions for the home that are elegantly simple, efficient and fun while reflecting the homeowner's personality and fulfilling his or her dream.

An award-winning interior designer, Brandi has established herself as a top interior designer in the Twin Cities. After 10 years with William Beson Interior Designs, she left the firm to open Eminent Interior Design, Ltd. and has amassed an impressive list of clientele that appreciate and seek Brandi's one-of-a-kind designs.

Much of Brandi's workload consists of new construction and remodeling, with many clients coming to her for help in material choices and creating furniture and architectural element layouts for new construction. When creating realistic layouts she works with the architects and the builders to create floor plans that function around the way that the clients will live within a given structure. Homeowners and clients should feel welcomed by their home; a home that "knows" them and was created just for them.

With every project, Brandi enjoys using "honest materials" to properly serve the design elements and philosophy she carries with her. The honest materials she favors are steel, wood, marble and glass. These natural elements always create interesting design with an unpredictable twist. Taking it a step further, she complements these hard elements with a comforting texture from all of her chosen fabrics.

With a kind confidence and inviting personality, Brandi emphasizes the value of a clear and open line of communication. Through a mutually respective relationship with their clients, the team at Eminent Design garners a level of expectation and a sense of vision that allows them to create unique homes, while respecting clients' dollars, that clients are proud to show friends and family. Above all, Brandi makes this design process something her clients view as a guided, fascinating journey of options, not a confusing list of stressful design decisions.

**ABOVE**
One side of twin vanities made from dark-stained mahogany topped with polished Pistachio Onyx. The vanity is complemented with a simple mirror and a mixture of Asian bronze and satin nickel finishes.
*Photograph by Trends Publishing International, Jamie Cobeldick*

**FACING PAGE**
Mixing the clients' contemporary taste with their Asian heritage makes this master bath truly unique. Custom-designed "Botanical Beach Grass" screen provides privacy and aesthetic appeal.
*Photograph by Trends Publishing International, Jamie Cobeldick*

Brandi patiently works to cater her designs to the needs of each of her clients by truly getting to know them, their lifestyles, personalities and desires. As she asserts, this is the only way to become a visionary and "advocate" for her clients. Many times they know what they don't like, but may not know where to begin with what they do like. Brandi wants "her homes" to reflect her clients and not appear as if a designer forced his or her style onto a room or home. Rather it should possess an air of having been developed over time. In many instances clients are surprised and thrilled by the final design as their open-mindedness and honesty allowed Brandi to venture into elements they hadn't initially envisioned for themselves, but had developed along the journey. It is this design journey that makes her designs neither predictable nor formulaic.

With every project, Brandi savors the opportunity to design a completely original space that looks and feels exactly like her clients. She is known for creating environments that evoke comfort and showcase good design for many years to come.

**TOP LEFT**
Neutral furniture creates a beautiful backdrop to accentuate the colorful rug and accent pillows.
*Photograph by LandMark Photography*

**BOTTOM LEFT**
This three-tiered island made from glass, granite and stainless steel works for cooking, cocktails or dinner for four.
*Photograph by LandMark Photography*

**FACING PAGE LEFT**
The clients' book collection is displayed in a dark-stained, custom-designed built-in with a tangerine backdrop.
*Photograph by Karen Melvin Photography*

**FACING PAGE RIGHT**
This downtown loft had the views but needed the color of the glass mosaic backsplash in the kitchen and warmth of the wool-and-silk rug in the living room.
*Photograph by Karen Melvin Photography*

# Q&A

## MORE ABOUT BRANDI ...

**WHAT PROJECT ARE YOU MOST PROUD OF?**

I am always completely enamored with whatever project I'm working on at the moment. I know that if I don't love it, my clients won't either. I design all my projects on that principle.

**WHAT IS THE HIGHEST COMPLIMENT THAT YOU HAVE RECEIVED PROFESSIONALLY?**

A client once said to me, "I can't believe you got into my head and got my house exactly how I envisioned it!"

**WHAT ELEMENT OF YOUR BUSINESS DO YOU FEEL YOUR CLIENTS FIND MOST VALUABLE?**

Eminent operates with the ease and experience of a larger firm but with the personal touch of a smaller company. We are flexible in how we work with each and every client.

EMINENT INTERIOR DESIGN, LTD.
Brandi Hagen
6478 Westchester Circle
Golden Valley, MN 55427
612.767.1242
Fax 612.767.1241
www.eminentid.com

# SUZANNE HAUGLAND
## DECORI DESIGNS

Serendipity often plays an important but inconspicuous role in the fated lives of artists, and Suzanne Haugland is no exception. Interested in the interior design field for the entirety of her life, she began as a flight attendant, and years ago she started an interior design business, quickly focusing all of her attention on making her passion a profitable business.

Always inspired by her own mother's interior design sense, after years of freelance work, Suzanne started her own retail shop that was geared mostly towards home accessories, but it kept evolving. Pretty soon she added furniture and then fabrics were added. Eventually, the store became a mini-design studio; the day after Labor Day 2006, she opened Decori Designs. Demolition of the existing building for redevelopment necessitated a move. The move inspired a new name that better encompassed the business.

Today, as you walk through the doors of Decori Designs you are greeted by Barney and Bailey, Suzanne's bearded collies, and you walk into a two-story, 7,000-square-foot retail furniture/fabric/accessories store/design studio with a big emphasis on design.

The creations Suzanne and Decori Designs specialize in are high-end residential interior designs that are what she likes to call "casually elegant"—interiors that are lovely, comfortable, livable and always beautiful. Suzanne and her team of designers can work with a client whether they are needing only one room re-worked or a whole house designed from the floor plan up.

When involved in new construction, Suzanne likes to be involved in the process from the blueprints on because she feels the end product will be a more cohesive and better-planned product when finished. Elements she tends to keep in mind on such projects are interior traffic-flow patterns, furniture and electrical outlet placement and other critical criteria

**ABOVE**
A hand-painted chest converted to a bathroom vanity dresses up a small bath.
*Photograph by Brian Bradshaw*

**FACING PAGE**
A Florida home of a Minneapolis family required the same bright colors and happy feel as their home in Minnesota. The Aubusson rug sets the color palette. Custom iron palm tree finials added the whimsical touch the homeowners enjoyed.
*Photograph by Greg Page*

that when worked out on the blueprints make it easier to avoid mistakes, thus saving money and time, which everyone can appreciate.

Suzanne and her team accomplish some wonderful interiors, all according to their clients' desires, needs and lifestyles. Clean lines and lifestyle-oriented designs are what could be considered Suzanne and her team's signature look, but ultimately she subscribes to the philosophy that function equals aesthetics, because in order for a home to be beautiful, it must function properly for the family who resides within the walls that shelter them.

Each spring and fall, Suzanne travels to High Point, North Carolina and to other markets during the year to look for specific pieces of furniture and other accessories for projects in the works. She goes to any length to find just the right

touches for each of her client's needs. When she travels to market, she takes a list of items she is looking for to complete her master creations. Sometimes when she feels she may have found exactly what a client is looking for while at market, she will take digital photographs and e-mail them to her client for approval.

Expanding her clients' creative awareness is priority for Suzanne and Decori Designs because a knowledgeable client is one who makes wise decisions. She acts as a teacher and guide by educating and then letting her clients give valuable input that steers a project into a home that is more reflective of their values and lifestyles than her own. This strategy allows for a more successful project that in the end pleases her clients because not only have they had the help of a skilled and dedicated professional, but they have also had a hand in it themselves.

Suzanne considers herself a conduit to intelligent designs and the wide variety of available products in the global market. She is the link to what the difference between a house and home can be for any family looking to improve their lives through a more functional and beautiful living environment.

**ABOVE**
The great room in a Minnesota lake home exhibits custom red cabinetry and red leather wing chairs. A carved mantel with a bear theme and bear border rug contribute to a Northern woodsy feel.
*Photograph by Brian Bradshaw*

**FACING PAGE LEFT**
Multiple arches and a tumbled-stone floor lead to the guest and sitting room.
*Photograph by Brian Bradshaw*

**FACING PAGE RIGHT**
The kitchen continues the bear theme with hand painting above cooking alcove and custom bear tiles on back splash. Painted bar stools add color to alder stained cabinetry.
*Photograph by Brian Bradshaw*

# MORE ABOUT SUZANNE ...

Q&A

### WHAT SEPARATES YOU FROM YOUR COMPETITION?

One of the things that we like to do when working with our clients is to have a good time at it. We want to enjoy the experience as much as we want them to enjoy it. We think that the process should be fun. It should be comfortable feeling, and in the end everyone should be thrilled with what they have accomplished. We are an easy group to work with. We feel our clients should have as much input as they can and be able to enjoy the whole experience.

### WHAT ELEMENT OF YOUR BUSINESS DO YOUR CLIENTS FEEL IS MOST VALUABLE?

I think they enjoy the resources that we have that are readily available to them and the fact that we are as excited about their project as they are.

### WHAT IS THE BEST PART OF BEING AN INTERIOR DESIGNER?

I enjoy everything. I've met some great people who have become my friends because I get so intimately involved with their lives for a year or two years while a project is getting built and furnished. I become a part of their lives.

### WHAT STYLE HAVE YOU RELIED ON FOR YEARS THAT STILL WORKS FOR YOU TODAY?

Comfortable. My designs need to be something that our clients walk into and say, "wow," but then they must be able to plop down into a chair. Even when we do a model home, we want people to be able to picture themselves sitting in that space, watching television and entertaining their friends. They need to feel that level of comfort.

DECORI DESIGNS
Suzanne Haugland
3924 West 50th Street
Edina, MN 55424
952.922.0111
Fax 952.922.3916

# DAVID HEIDE
## DAVID HEIDE DESIGN STUDIO

David Heide Design Studio bases its design philosophy on following historic precedent while meeting modern needs. The result is a rich tapestry of historically accurate designs that flow gracefully from the exterior through to the interior.

The Studio's design work pays homage to historic character while simultaneously incorporating contemporary conveniences and comforts—the firm considers houses to be works in progress rather than artifacts and believes that a residence must evolve over time to fit the habits of its owners. When starting a new project, the Studio begins by considering the current or anticipated function of a building and then seeking out the appropriate design elements to suit this need. They examine and document the existing building, looking for visual cues signaling the original design elements and considering ways to utilize these elements in the design of the remodeled or new space, and they also conduct research into the intended or established style of the residence using their extensive library, as well as resources relating to the particular project, such as historic photos or documents.

In addition to restoration and remodeling projects, the Studio also designs new homes in period styles, among them a large lake cottage in northern Minnesota that was inspired by the work of Greene & Greene, in the aesthetic of the Arts & Crafts tradition. All designs, from the millwork, stencil details, handmade tiles and range hood to the custom light fixtures accenting the design of the structure, were created by the Studio.

After earning a Bachelor of Architecture degree from Drake University and pursuing graduate studies at the University of Minnesota and the Minneapolis College of Art and Design, David Heide joined the Minneapolis firm MacDonald & Mack Architects. During his 11-year tenure, he worked on a wide variety of historic preservation projects, including residences, churches, courthouses and other municipal buildings. He departed in 1997 to found David Heide Design Studio, which offers both architectural and interior design services.

The greatest lesson David has learned from his career is that good projects are a melding together of many talented people, on behalf of the client, with the best possible design work to create a final masterpiece. He applies this lesson by listening to and learning from every

**ABOVE & FACING PAGE**
This new lake cottage abounds in Arts & Crafts details. The leaf-print textile frieze alludes to the surrounding forest while cleverly concealing the sound system's speakers. Careful material selection and thoughtful design create a space that is at once organized and inviting. Day beds with trundle beds are separated by cabinets for storage.
*Photographs by Karen Melvin*

person involved with the project, from the client to the construction crew, and by creating a true studio environment within the firm. Their work is the product of many talented people working together to create beautiful, innovative designs. The end result of this process, David has realized, is superior to what it would be if he tried to direct the whole thing himself.

David strongly believes in the synthesis of architecture and interior design. This separates the Studio from other firms in the area—everything you see in their projects was designed by the David Heide Design Studio team, including, in many cases, light fixtures and custom handmade tile and stencils, and in most cases these items are fabricated specifically for their clients, often locally.

When working in a historic context, David prides himself on the fact that the Studio does not copy works from the past or create a false sense of historicism—they bring together people who know and understand historic building technology and historic building techniques, whether it's the design of millwork or cabinetry.

David Heide Design Studio has been awarded the 2005 ASID Award for Historic Preservation, the 2004 Minneapolis HPC Award for a New Addition to a Historic Building, the 2003 Minneapolis HPC Award for Rehabilitation, the 2003 ASID Award for Kitchen Design, a Sub-Zero/Wolf Kitchen Design Award and numerous others.

**TOP LEFT**
With custom-made cabinetry, a mosaic encaustic tile floor and windows overlooking a magnificent garden, this breakfast room creates a pastoral environment in a historic urban home.
*Photograph by Karen Melvin*

**BOTTOM LEFT**
A newly remodeled kitchen recreates many historic details of the house, while discreetly adding modern amenities and subtle design flourishes in cherry cabinetry.
*Photograph by Karen Melvin*

**FACING PAGE**
A streamlined Art Deco look for this remodeled kitchen evokes the historic roots of the house while giving this central gathering space a warm, inviting feel.
*Photograph by Alex Steinberg*

**ABOVE**
New built-in cabinetry, custom-made art glass, refined furnishings and dramatic window treatments make this once-mundane dining room the centerpiece of this historic house.
*Photograph by Karen Melvin*

**FACING PAGE LEFT**
From the light fixtures to the wall finishes, every detail of this bathroom remodeling respects and reflects the historic nature of this 1890's house.
*Photograph by Karen Melvin*

**FACING PAGE RIGHT**
Modern-inspired furnishings act as a counterpoint to the rich, historically informed Art Deco-styled custom cabinetry and woodwork; this family room is a showcase of contrasting yet complementary styles.
*Photograph by Alex Steinberg*

# MORE ABOUT DAVID ...

Q&A

WHAT SINGLE THING WOULD YOU DO TO BRING A DULL HOUSE
TO LIFE?

Move into it.

WHAT IS THE BEST PART OF BEING A DESIGNER?

I have my dream job. If I could be doing anything, I would choose this.

WHAT IS THE MOST UNUSUAL DESIGN THAT YOU'VE USED IN ONE OF
YOUR PROJECTS?

Much of the work we do is custom. Whether we design light fixtures, tile, art glass or

furniture, we are always incorporating the decorative arts into our work.

DAVID HEIDE DESIGN STUDIO
David Heide, AIA Associate, Allied Member ASID
663 Grain Exchange Building, 301 Fourth Avenue South
Minneapolis, MN 55415
612.337.5060
Fax 612.337.5059
www.dhdstudio.com

# KIMBERLY HERRICK
## HERRICK DESIGN GROUP

Guided and grounded by a successful philosophy, Kimberly Herrick, founder of Herrick Design Group, believes in the power of little lessons learned every single day. And the greatest lesson is the ability to store that information for the future situations life is sure to present. Most importantly: never stop looking for or learning from those lessons.

Upon reflection, it is apparent Kimberly has always been interested in the field of interior design. After graduating from the University of Minnesota with an interior design degree, she began working with a large, prestigious firm in downtown Minneapolis. She used the valuable experience and years spent there learning about the industry to further develop and sharpen her skills. She knew the next most logical step was to strike out on her own, which she did in 2003.

Since its debut, Herrick Design Group has developed a long list of impressed and grateful clients. From residential new construction, remodels to interior/exterior architectural palettes, Kimberly directs her clients based on their cues. She listens thoughtfully and learns to "read" her clients: interpreting body language and facial expression oftentimes leads to the underlying meaning of the spoken words. The design business is about building relationships, and Kimberly knows that when her clients invite and trust her to enter their lives, it is no small gesture.

Kimberly seeks inspiration in elements that are not necessarily in the built environment or directly correlated to interiors. For example, architecture can be a springboard for a cabinet; a color one might observe in a piece of clothing just might be the perfect palette in a bedroom; a stone may fittingly complement a particular wood type within a client's

**ABOVE**
Japanese artifacts take center stage in this master bedroom where elegant taupes and grays are the rule.
*Photograph by Stuart M. Herrick*

**FACING PAGE**
Contrast is key in this lyrically inspired living room, as is evidenced by the plush mohair sofa opposite the black lacquer of the baby grand piano.
*Photograph by Stuart M. Herrick*

current furnishings. It is this ability to see beyond an element's immediate value that also assists in her ability to envision an empty room furnished to the last accessory.

If she had to describe her style, Kimberly would rather give examples of what she thinks encompasses good design. She enjoys contrasts, such as the juxtaposition of matte and shiny surfaces, hard and soft textures, masculine and feminine touches and countless other combinations. Although a true believer in new adaptations of old forms, Kimberly doesn't rely on past projects. The idea is to surround a space with the homeowner's identity. She prides herself on always searching for original answers to each client's unique situation, rather than relying solely on the safety net of a successful past design. To that end, she is not afraid to experiment or push herself creatively to find the answer.

Above all, the home must be livable and tailored to the particular family's everyday living habits. As the busy mother of three and the sole proprietor of her own firm, Kimberly is all too familiar with the idea of having a home that works for its owners and she is only too thankful for the opportunity to create these outstanding environments.

**TOP LEFT**
The leather tile applied to the fireplace walls in a herringbone fashion anchors this modern Englishman's gallery.
*Photograph by Stuart M. Herrick*

**BOTTOM LEFT**
A dining room with sisal wall covering perfectly envelops this client's mid-century Danish dining suite.
*Photograph by Stuart M. Herrick*

**FACING PAGE**
This modern media room with strong lines and inviting seating welcomes the theatrically savvy.
*Photograph by Stuart M. Herrick*

# MORE ABOUT KIMBERLY ...

**Q&A**

WHAT IS YOUR MOST VALUABLE BUSINESS ATTRIBUTE?

It's the confidence that we are making the *right* decisions. Many times our clients are putting every ounce of trust in our choices. We are responsible for that trust and take it very seriously.

HAS TRAVEL INFLUENCED YOUR DESIGNS?

Yes, definitely. I always look at architecture for inspiration wherever I go. The different references, color palettes, styles and just the way people live throughout the world is always inspiration for me. In the Midwest we think of space differently than people in New York. Space is very much defined by geographic location.

HERRICK DESIGN GROUP
Kimberly Herrick
19180 Poplar Circle, Suite 102
Minneapolis, MN 55347
952.220.5958
Fax 952.906.3090

# SUSAN HOFFMAN

## DESIGNS!

For many homeowners, selecting an interior designer is a personal, even intense task. Finding the right person who can help you make the best choices for your style needs is a challenge. Susan Hoffman's reputation has been earned over years of creative service to her clients. "Susan Hoffman helped me" are words that many have said with pride and credibility.

Susan's interior design business, DESIGNS!, works with clients all over the country, creating interior design solutions. She is well known for mastering construction complexities, whether new construction or remodeling. She works closely with builders, architects and even tradespeople to ensure that her clients receive the best job for the money. "She pre-empts errors before they get implemented," said one client recently. "She translated the plans for us and worked hard to make sure the plans fit our lifestyle even better."

DESIGNS! is a well-recognized, full-service design studio in Wayzata, Minnesota. Her showroom, P.O.S.H. (Property of Susan Hoffman), is located close by in Plymouth, Minnesota. With countless samples in her design studio and a substantial inventory of accessories and furniture in her showroom, DESIGNS!'s clients find comfort in their ability to find the right sample or product at the right time.

The sample library at DESIGNS! is one of the largest in the Twin Cities. Susan's relationships with vendors reflect her outstanding credibility and reputation—she simply has more of the latest in room finishes and other products so that her clients have the widest range of selections right in her own office. This makes the entire process more convenient and faster. Her process streamlines the project; ultimately, of course saving her clients time and money.

Susan is committed to providing quality design to anyone and works on projects from small to large. The staff at DESIGNS! can manage projects from start to finish. Susan and her team of ASID interior designers and qualified staff have the requisite experience to make any design project more productive ... and fun.

**ABOVE**
Private residence.
*Photograph by Brian Droege/MSP*

**FACING PAGE**
People's Choice Award–winning and Designers' Choice Award–winner ASID Showcase Home, designed in conjunction with staff designers Judy McCaffney, ASID and Leah Fasching, ASID.
*Photograph by Karen Melvin/MSP*

**ABOVE**
Private residence.
*Photograph by Chuck Carver*

**LEFT**
ASID Showcase Home.
*Photograph by Doug Wong/MSP*

**FACING PAGE LEFT**
ASID Showcase Home in conjunction with staff designers Judy McCaffrey, ASID and Leah Fasching, ASID.
*Photograph by Karen Melvin/MSP*

**FACING PAGE RIGHT**
Cramer Luxury Home/ Private residence designed in conjunction with Leah Fasching, ASID-staff designer.
*Photograph by Landmark Photography/MN Monthly*

# MORE ABOUT SUSAN ...

## Q&A

**WHO HAS HAD THE BIGGEST INFLUENCE ON YOUR CAREER?**

My husband, who is also an entrepreneur. Not in a design sense, but more in a business sense. He has been very encouraging and very willing to support me when I take chances. He always gives me great advice when I've asked for it.

**WHAT ELEMENTS OF YOUR BUSINESS DO YOUR CLIENTS FIND MOST VALUABLE?**

Our attention to detail, our knowledge of resources and our trying to make it as smooth for them as possible.

**WHAT IS THE MOST REWARDING PART OF BEING AN INTERIOR DESIGNER?**

I would say the best part is constantly being faced with new challenges and new adventures. Creating new things all of the time is the most rewarding part.

DESIGNS!
SUSAN HOFFMAN INTERIOR DESIGNS
Susan Hoffman
317 East Wayzata Boulevard
Wayzata, MN 55391
952.475.0196
Fax 952.475.0593
www.susanhoffman.com

# JULIE ANN JOHNSON
## JULIAN INTERIORS AND DESIGN

The philosophy of "shaping the art of living" permeates Julie Ann Johnson's designs. Drawing on her innate talent for making people feel at home, Julie Ann focuses on creating spaces that people really live in and use. This focus paved the way for Julian Interiors and Design, the firm she built from a mere idea in Roseau, Minnesota, to a nine-person company operating in Wayzata, Minnesota. Over the years, Julie Ann has continued her dedication to designing lifestyle-friendly environments that remain timeless, personal, functional and as aesthetically pleasing as when they were completed.

Julie Ann entered the world of design over 28 years ago with her first job selling furniture to her small, northern hometown of Roseau. Julie Ann had found her passion in the world of interior design and from the start had an instinctive and organic sense of style that she fed with her studies of history, art and Old World architecture. Her passions soon outgrew her hometown, and she moved to the Twin Cities where she opened a large home center that has become nationally recognized as one of America's major style setters.

Julie Ann has since moved to her new locale in Wayzata, housed in a showroom overlooking beautiful Lake Minnetonka. Since its inception, Julian Interiors and Design has grown into a full-service design business replete with a broad network of business associates with whom Julie Ann closely works. As a result of these connections, she can provide every client with a vast array of unique items including custom draperies, floor coverings, exclusive interior and exterior architectural work, Italian glasswork and one-of-a-kind antiques. Fine artwork is a cornerstone to Julie Ann's designs, and Julian Interiors is a distributor for a number of nationally and internationally recognized artists. As a testament to her skills, Julie Ann's strong client following is largely due to referrals from prior patrons, many of whom remain

**ABOVE**
The space employs state-of-the-art conveniences from the 21st century and maintains the threads of history that define the design's vision.
*Photograph by Landmark Photography*

**FACING PAGE**
Inspired by "Sunroom," a painting by Schall, the conservatory is a peaceful space that invites the outdoors into the home.
*Photograph by Dana Wheelock Photography*

close friends. Together with her team, Julie Ann designs high-end residential and commercial interiors. Their designs have been featured in *Better Homes and Gardens*, on the cover of *Midwest Home* and elsewhere.

Despite her company's evolution, Julie Ann's mission remains the same: To "shape the art of living" by combining an opulent combination of styles to create spaces that bring people together and stand the test of time. Julie Ann and her team work hand in hand with architects, builders and artisans and believe that design is a process and not an event. Before ever stepping into a

**ABOVE**
Simplicity and elegance coexist in this room to create a quiet reflective space, inviting and peaceful.
*Photograph by Dana Wheelock Photography*

**RIGHT**
The classical dining room is designed to function as a formal dining area and library. The magnificent carved bookcases feature rich mahogany paneling and shelving. The gracious circular line of the room echoes the Oscar de la Renta radial expansion table from Century Furniture.
*Photograph by Dana Wheelock Photography*

**FACING PAGE**
Family and friends, luxury and ease, simplicity and grandeur: The anticipation of what lies around the corner and the excitement of its discovery define this space.
*Photograph by Dana Wheelock Photography*

family's home, she meets with them to get to know their personalities and get a fundamental understanding of their needs and likes. It is Julie Ann's belief that the designer's purpose is not to reinvent the past; rather, it is to interpret and apply it in a modern way. She does this by adding an antique door on a closet or creating unique focal points, such as a custom fireplace or an artisan-finished wall. Throughout the process, Julie Ann and her team remain committed to enriching their clients' lives through design.

Julie Ann invokes intimacy in her showroom, as well. Her intuitive design sense and love of beautiful things are reflected in her concentrated, timeless collection. Walk through the showroom doors and you will likely run into friends admiring lamps, rugs and other furnishings or maybe just having a chat with Billie, Julie Ann's daughter and business partner. You will probably even be invited to one of the many events Julie Ann holds at her showroom. Whatever your experience or reason for visiting, you will leave with the overwhelming sense that Julian Interiors and Design is engaged in shaping the art of living and can help you define your sense of home.

# MORE ABOUT JULIE ANN ...

### YOU WOULD NOT KNOW IT, BUT MY FRIENDS WOULD TELL YOU ...

That I am an inspired woman. That I am honest, modest and rely on universal guidance to help lead me through my business and personal life. They would also share with you that I love animals and am trained in classical horse riding.

### YOU CAN TELL I LIVE IN THIS LOCALE BECAUSE ...

I rely on Midwestern rules of business. Here, a person's word is his contract, honesty and frank communication are appreciated and hard work is rewarded. Midwesterners place a high price on time and values. As a firm, we have endeavored to embody all of this.

### DESCRIBE YOUR STYLE OR DESIGN PREFERENCES.

Our designs typically reflect a European influence. We are not in the business of reinventing, but we like to interpret and apply classic ideas in modern ways.

*Photograph by Amy Jeanchaiyaphum*

### JULIAN INTERIORS AND DESIGN
Julie Ann Johnson
294 Grove Lane East, Suite 150
Wayzata, MN 55391
952.249.6253
Fax 952.249.6254

**ABOVE**
This room exemplifies one of the French and Italian design fundamentals: Harmony is far more important than conformity.
*Photograph by Landmark Photography*

**FACING PAGE**
Our clients are dimensional. Their experience gives them layers. They value the art of living.
*Photograph by Dana Wheelock Photography*

# KARA A. KARPENSKE

## KAMARRON DESIGN, INC.

K ara A. Karpenske is coveted by clients both for her beautiful design ideas and for her business acumen. Beginning her professional life in international business, she traveled abroad eight months a year, an experience that proved incredibly beneficial to her later in life. While she experienced great success as a businesswoman, she always carried with her a love and innate talent for interior design. Her knack for creating beautiful interior spaces was widely recognized and commented on by friends. In 2001, Kara decided to integrate her passion with her business sense to create Kamarron Design, Inc., the firm she now runs with the help of three assistants and a 10-person installation crew.

Kara credits her ability to earn her clients' trust for her incredible success. Her innovative ideas and ability to work with their budgets, needs and often differing tastes to create designs that work in every regard garners a strong following of loyal patrons, both residential and commercial. So, too, does her incredible business sense. Kara devises a plan for all of her clients, helping them map out a design trajectory whereby they can add design elements over time, as their budgets allow. In so doing, she helps steer her clients toward good investments

and helps them avoid simply filling up space with less desirable items. Her background in business also helps her as she works with dealers and craftspeople to facilitate projects. She serves as a mentor for other designers, helping them to understand that regardless of how creative one is, one must also know how to channel that energy to effectively and efficiently accomplish design goals.

Kara describes her design preference as "classic with a twist," further explaining that she tends toward universally appealing lines and shapes but peppers them with surprising touches. Having traveled extensively to Mexico, Puerto Rico, Spain and other various exotic

**ABOVE**
A tight-backed settee paired with an ornate round mirror and antique Chinese stools creates a unique look for this modest Coon Rapids home.
*Photograph by Phillip Mueller*

**FACING PAGE**
This dynamic dining room was styled for an Excelsior family who sought to meld two distinctive styles to create a timeless yet functional enviroment. Their home, designated to Historic Excelsior registry, had its own history, which they wished to capture along with the couple's love for a modern flow. Kara used a historic color palette, candlebra candalier and tufted paisley chairs combined with, modern, striped window treatments and a contempary table to create this sophisticated room.
*Photograph by Bill Diers Photography*

locations, she infuses her designs with international flavor by way of unique furniture pieces, silks and other unexpected items and materials. For example, she enjoys adding rustic elements to a modern room or Asian-inspired accent tables in an otherwise traditional setting. It is her confidence that allows Kara to successfully execute these extraordinary additions. She believes in her intuition, and her conviction is contagious. Patrons skeptical about suggestions become fully assured when Kara places pieces in their rooms. As a result, they quickly develop a strong faith in her talent for interpreting their desires in an exciting way.

Such instances of her design innovations include a bathroom she refurbished in an existing home. Striving to stay within the client's allotted budget but also bring new life to the dull space, Kara found the perfect wall ornaments: inexpensive bamboo placemats. Her clients were slightly taken aback at the suggestion, but the presentation convinced them that Kara's out-of-the-box idea was right on target. For another project, Kara was charged to find a bed for a couple's master bedroom that both suited the woman's very feminine sensibility and remained sensitive to the gentleman's masculine taste. Clients of Kara's for more than three years, the couple had grown to

**TOP RIGHT**
Kamarron Design, Inc. created pure elegance in this North Oaks great room. A traditional brick fireplace is anchored by bold, striped window panels and original oil artwork. A grand sofa is enveloped in a leather shell and soft chenille damask cushions. The classic chairs are timeless in the teal-accented, gold-medallion patterned fabric.
*Photograph by Phillip Mueller*

**BOTTOM RIGHT**
A mixture of subtle patterns adds interest to this small space. The traditional chest of drawers is flanked by modern topiaries, allowing the patterns to work. Attention to detail in the accessories shows in the lamps and hand-forged candlesticks.
*Photograph by Phillip Mueller*

**FACING PAGE**
Seaside-hue blue and a touch of warm gold help create the warm and inviting ambience in this guest room. The elegant antique crystal chandelier adds a distinctive flair while the black and white artwork helps enhance the feeling of invitation.
*Photograph by Phillip Mueller*

understand that what they saw as irreconcilable differences, Kara embraced as an exhilarating challenge. They gave her the reins, and Kara found a Queen Anne–style headboard that was covered with leather and studded with nails—a perfect compromise of delicate style with strong, rugged materials.

Kara's knack for interior artistry is no secret. Serving as a co-vice president on IFDA's board of directors, she is well known by her peers as a vibrant member of the design community. Her projects have been featured in *Midwest Home, Mpls. St. Paul Magazine* and *Furnishings* and have earned her local renown when rooms she designed won awards as public favorites in 2004 and 2005. She is known not only for her work in Minneapolis/St. Paul but for homes she has designed in Austin, South Padre Island and Washington, D.C., and she will soon begin projects in Las Vegas and New Orleans. But for Kara, the greatest source of pride and satisfaction comes from her clients' unwavering trust and friendship.

**TOP LEFT**
From dusk to dawn, this suburban couple enjoys their master suite. The brown leather and nailheads add a masculine stamp on an otherwise feminine Queen Anne-style headboard. Damask silk window treatments topped with an organic plaid ground this warm and comfortable master bedroom.
*Photograph by Phillip Mueller*

**BOTTOM LEFT**
Home is where the heart is, and so is this kitchen for a North Oaks family. The homeowners and their two small children relish in the attention to detail found in this intimate area. Full-movement granite flows seamlessly on the large traditional island. Attention to detail is clear in the slate backsplash, light fixtures and accessories. A cozy niche is created with two french bordeaux chairs, making a place for all of the family to relax and entertain.
*Photograph by Phillip Mueller*

**FACING PAGE LEFT**
To maximize space in this master bathroom, every square inch was considered, from the custom vanity to the tile work. This Blaine homeowner sought a spa-like experience with an open feeling. The heavy glass shower doors and use of textured walls help elevate this bathroom to a sanctuary.
*Photograph by Phillip Mueller*

**FACING PAGE RIGHT**
A modern mix of stainless steel appliances, recessed panel cabinetry and glass tile in the kitchen adds daily delight for the Excelsior couple who reside in this home. A cup of coffee is easily enjoyed under the modern track lighting fixture sporting onyx glass. An olive-hued green used on the wall complements the large, natural slate bowl atop the island.
*Photograph by Bill Diers Photography*

# Q&A

# MORE ABOUT KARA ...

IF YOU COULD ELIMINATE ONE DESIGN STYLE FROM THE WORLD, WHAT WOULD IT BE?

I wouldn't eliminate any styles. Every style appeals and applies to some client—and it's the client's preferences that matter in design.

YOU CAN TELL I LIVE IN THIS LOCALE BECAUSE ...

I'm genuine and nice—classic Minnesota traits.

WHAT IS THE HIGHEST ACCOMPLISHMENT YOU'VE ACHIEVED PROFESSIONALLY?

Receiving the people's choice awards two years in a row. To have my designs chosen as the best by the public means more to me than any other honor could!

MY FRIENDS WOULD TELL YOU I AM ...

Quite a comedienne! I play jokes on my clients, bringing them outlandish pieces that I don't intend to use just to give them a laugh. I really like to bring fun into my life and my work.

KAMARRON DESIGN, INC.
Kara A. Karpenske, IFDA
11814 South Lake Boulevard Northeast
Blaine, MN 55449
612.396.1840
Fax 952.403.6982
www.kamarrondesign.com

# JENNIE KORSBON

## KR DESIGN

Jennie Korbson, partner in KR Design, stands apart from other interior designers in the area with her fresh ideas, her keen "eye" and her highly creative way of approaching projects. Her clients feel that her most valuable asset is her ability to interpret their needs as well as desires within whatever vernacular her clients dream.

A graduate of the interior design program at the University of Wisconsin-Stout, Jennie feels her studio-based education is invaluable, and today it plays a vital part in her day-to-day business. This critical education gave her a trained eye in which to see art and express its value to her clients.

While her business focuses on residential, including high-end new construction and remodels, she has also been invited to design numerous offices spaces. She incorporates contemporary influences in many of her projects with the use of eclectic accessories and beautiful artwork, including modernistic sculptures and imported Asian busts. Jennie

enthusiastically tackles any undertaking commissioned, bringing her trained eye, fresh approach and enthusiasm no matter the scope or budget. Jennie feels that when she takes on a new client, she sees herself as her client's advocate, ensuring that all options have been presented by suggesting ideas that the client did not even know were available. Jennie feels it is part of her vocation to educate her clients about their endless options.

Jennie prides herself in her ability to nurture a project from the blueprint stage all the way to the final details of new construction, remodeling or redecorating an existing space. Her

**ABOVE**
The handmade French secretary adds height to the room, as well a place to store the client's treasures. The Bergere chairs offer a burst of intense color.
*Photograph by Alex Steinberg*

**FACING PAGE**
The living room has a spacious yet cozy feel with lofty ceilings and a large, colorful antique rug. The sofas provide a neutral palette for all of the accents of color in the room.
*Photograph by Alex Steinberg*

clients adore her designs and her beautiful attention to detail. With a client-driven look, Jennie feels that listening to her clients' vision is the key to her success. She strives to work in a wide array of styles by addressing and interpreting her clients' needs, desires and what will ultimately work best for her clients' family and lifestyle. Her goal is to make her clients not only comfortable, but proud of the homes in which they live.

Whatever look Jennie's clients demand, she can find it, make it and/or design it in a timely manner and to an absolute, beautiful "tee." And no matter the scope of a project, she is proud and honored to improve her clients' day-to-day living through her unique design solutions.

**TOP LEFT**
The dining room boasts an original Jamali and glitzy gold leather chairs. The client picked out the chandelier on a trip to Italy.
*Photograph by Alex Steinberg*

**BOTTOM LEFT**
The symmetry of the room gives a sense of order. Metallic finishes on the accessories and drapery give the room a shimmery quality.
*Photograph by Alex Steinberg*

**FACING PAGE LEFT**
This is a quiet spot for the homeowner. It has been personalized with her initials, which are surrounded by an oval ring of rhinestones. The drapery has been pulled back with a custom crystal tieback.
*Photograph by Alex Steinberg*

**FACING PAGE RIGHT**
The idea for this space was to create a room for reflecting while taking in the beautiful lake view. The updated Asian theme is simple and fun.
*Photograph by Alex Steinberg*

# MORE ABOUT JENNIE ...

## Q&A

### WHAT IS THE BEST PART OF BEING AN INTERIOR DESIGNER?

It is seeing the look on my clients' faces after everything is installed. I especially love to install everything all in the same day so there is a big impact. I love watching them touch every surface and watching them find all of the fun secrets of each piece of furniture.

### WHAT IS THE HIGHEST COMPLIMENT THAT YOU HAVE RECEIVED PROFESSIONALLY?

The thing that I hear most often that makes me beam is that I am "up and coming." That gives me confidence and makes me feel so good because I hear compliments from clients all of the time, but when they come from my peers it means that people are recognizing me . That takes a while when you are in this industry.

### WHAT IS YOUR STUDIO LIKE?

My studio is based out of Minnetonka. It is an intimate studio with a few furniture settings, vintage plank floors and other interesting architectural details. It is a joy to come to work every day to a space that is both comforting and inspiring.

### WHAT WILL THE FUTURE HOLD FOR KR DESIGN?

I would like to be doing more projects in different parts of the country.

KR DESIGN
Jennie Korsbon
3319 Highway 101 South
Minnetonka, MN 55391
952.473.4440
Fax 952.473.0225

# CYNTHIA LARSON

## CYNTHIA LARSON INTERIOR DESIGN

Cynthia treats her design projects like a painting. And as a painter herself, she understands that this process is never quite finished. With this in mind, Cynthia works to tailor her clients' interiors to their lifestyles and help them see themselves therein so that they can pick up where she leaves off and continue to add to and transform their living spaces.

Cynthia's design background stretches back as far as childhood. Her parents, attuned to aesthetics, built their home to model one of Frank Lloyd Wright's designs. Perhaps sensing a predilection in her daughter for things visual, Cynthia's mother allowed the preschooler to make the final selection for her bedroom's theme and was impressed with the sophistication of her choice.

Cynthia continued to enhance and refine her artistic skill throughout her adolescence and young adulthood, eventually attending the Minneapolis College of Art and Design in the 1970s—the heyday of conceptual art. She graduated with a fine arts degree and studied painting for one year in London before returning to Massachusetts with the intent to complete her education in architecture at Harvard Graduate School of Design. However, she ultimately decided that she preferred interior spaces to exterior structures, deferred her enrollment and pursued the design profession instead, later attending Parsons School of Design in New York City.

Her first design project set her on a steady career trajectory. Working for a small architectural firm in Cambridge, Massachusetts, Cynthia joined the team in rebuilding the Jordan Pond House in Maine's Acadia National Park, a home on land donated to the National Park Service by John D. Rockefeller Jr. Having burned to the ground, the tea house needed to

**ABOVE**
French glass doors open on an airy master bedroom hallway. The large mirror and antique chandelier—a family heirloom—emphasize the natural light, and the raspberry wallpaper provides warmth.
*Photograph by David McMahon*

**FACING PAGE**
The large bay window of this Lake Minnetonka home's living room provides a spectacular view. A beautiful Brazilian cherry floor and built-in cherry cabinets flanking the fireplace underscore the high cherry-beamed ceiling. The large-scale furniture, including a custom-made Italian sofa table with beautiful inlay, offsets the ceiling height and weight of the fireplace, and dark woods and cocoa-colored walls add warmth.
*Photograph by David McMahon*

be completely rebuilt and restored. The team's completed design won a Progressive Architecture award and set the stage for what was to become Cynthia's incredibly successful design career.

While she worked as a corporate interior designer for many years, Cynthia now focuses on new residential construction and renovations with her solo practice, Cynthia Larson Interior Design, which she founded in 1990. Unlike many interior designers, Cynthia is proud to refer to herself as a decorator. Having spent many years at construction sites, she has grown increasingly passionate about the finishing stages of a residence—adding wall color, floor coverings, furniture and accessories, those final touches that bring a home to life.

Describing her style as one of comfort with touches of a Southern European style, Cynthia incorporates a few modern elements into an otherwise classic interior landscape. She lends a thoughtful, international flair to each home she designs, and her two ASID awards speak to the success with which she does so. While she continues to paint avidly, she feels blessed to make her living through her innate talent for realizing clients' artistic desires for their homes.

**TOP LEFT**
The dining room set in the designer's home is an Althorp House reproduction, and the chairs are made more luxurious with French tapestry upholstery by Clarence House. The silk draperies and gold-colored walls add warmth to the room, and soft lighting emanates from Fortuny sconces and a French wrought-iron chandelier.
*Photograph by David McMahon*

**BOTTOM LEFT**
The living room of this Country French-influenced home features a carved stone fireplace, fauxed, sunset-color walls and reminders of the client's trips to the Caribbean. Patterns of birds, flowers and raspberries appear in the fabrics and the rug.
*Photograph by David McMahon*

**FACING PAGE LEFT**
This breakfast room features a 19th-century table and primitive New England chairs. Bright-yellow antique Italian dishes complement the Fortuny light fixture above.
*Photograph by David McMahon*

**FACING PAGE RIGHT**
An Amy Howard antique-style mirrored chest in this guestroom suite designed for the ASID Showhouse displays a Chinese statue and glass fruit. The bright floral bouquet accentuates the watercolor reproduction of a Cézanne painting.
*Photograph by David McMahon*

# MORE ABOUT CYNTHIA ...

**Q&A**

NAME ONE THING MOST PEOPLE DON'T KNOW ABOUT YOU.

People are very surprised when I mention that I did a 30-day Outward Bound expedition. I loved the opportunity to push my limits and rely on others to get by. It truly taught me that I am capable of accomplishing anything. I continue to feed my love of the outdoors with hiking outings out West and kayaking sojourns to Canada.

WHAT COLOR BEST DESCRIBES YOU AND WHY?

I love the yellow one finds in wheat fields. As I am of Swedish and Danish descent, my hair is almost the same color. Yellow is light and happy, and it just feels like me.

WHAT IS THE MOST MEMORABLE PROJECT YOU'VE BEEN INVOLVED WITH?

About 15 years ago, I was the interior decorator for a home of a client who had lived in Asia and China and collected many antiques from the area. His architect had been his childhood best friend and would have been in my graduating class at the Harvard Graduate School of Design, had I chosen to attend. He had restored a 1920's home for the client, raising the ceilings to accommodate his enormous Chinese cupboards. I was privileged to work with two gentlemen who had such knowledge and appreciation of Fortuny lighting, beautiful textiles and amazing stone and granite. It was an incredible education and certainly my most memorable experience.

CYNTHIA LARSON INTERIOR DESIGN
Cynthia Larson, Allied Member ASID
Wayzata, MN
612.339.2226

# JOHN LASSILA

## JOHN LASSILA & ASSOCIATES, LTD.

Hailing from a long line of entrepreneurial-minded family members and with a quarter of a century's worth of practical experience in interior design, John Lassila demonstrates his passion for beautiful rooms and extensive knowledge of the interior design field within John Lassila & Associates, Ltd., the Minneapolis firm he founded 10 years ago.

John does not subscribe to one particular style; rather, he achieves a definite feeling of warmth, comfort, livability and personality through his designs by listening to his clients. In this day and age, John knows people's lives have become so hectic that in contrast, the spirit of their home should create solace from a demanding day and offer a nurturing environment.

The firm primarily addresses residential design and a wide body of work can be appreciated in homes in Minnesota and Chicago, Florida, Hilton Head Island and the Napa Valley. Although the firm maintains quite an impressive list of projects, John prefers the firm to stay small, grounded. He enjoys the personal interaction and hands-on approach clients have come to expect when seeking his firm's designs. As a result, business is plentiful and much comes from repeat clients and pleased referrals.

**LEFT**
A simple color palette creates dynamic contrast in the lounge area of this lower-level media room. Asian, Art Deco and classic-styled pieces combine in an exciting mix.
*Photograph by Alex Steinberg*

John Lassila & Associates, Ltd. offers its clients the convenience of a design studio and showroom with all the benefits of its wealth of national and international resources. The studio supports John's philosophy that accessories and art are critical to a space's overall success. Further developing that idea, John stresses the importance of personalizing spaces with objects such as family mementos and collections that hold special meaning for the homeowner.

It is John's ability of envisioning a room's completed look before even beginning which never fails to awe his clients. The potential he sees when he walks into a space always materializes in the most astounding ways. In this way, the team at John Lassila & Associates, Ltd. not only specializes in making over spaces with furniture and fabric selections, they create total environments, with extensive experience in renovation and new construction consultation. From custom cabinetry to carpet selection, the firm guides lasting room design grounded by special pieces throughout. And although a room and all of its components may be new,

John strives to make it appear as if it has always been so, and that is the true test of an interior designer.

Always forward-thinking and never one to sit complacent, John dreams of opening a retail shop filled with the kind of furnishings, art and objects that mirror his design work. Much like any of his clients will tell you, if he dreams it, he will make it happen.

**ABOVE LEFT**
An illuminated barrel vault with a Regency-styled pendant adds drama to this corridor leading to a master suite. The existing wood floor was embellished with a faux marbre painted design in the classical style.
*Photograph by Alex Steinberg*

**ABOVE RIGHT**
French Country details including hand-wrought iron, painted finishes and distressed woods offer a warm, inviting atmosphere in this kitchen.
*Photograph by Alex Steinberg*

**FACING PAGE**
Furnishings in numerous styles harmonize with one another via a monochromatic color palette in this multi-purpose space. Wall finishes and fabrics were kept light to offset the room's dark millwork.
*Photograph by Alex Steinberg*

# MORE ABOUT JOHN ...

## Q&A

**WHAT SEPARATES YOU FROM YOUR COMPETITION?**

It's the level of detail that I strive to do in every project whether it is a room or two, or a large construction project. I believe in the importance of accessories, art and personal mementos that bring a high level of completion to a project. Not all designers take projects down to quite that level.

**WHAT IS THE HIGHEST COMPLIMENT YOU'VE EVER RECEIVED?**

The end of a project when our clients comment that everything feels like it has always been there. Though everything may be brand new we strive to create rooms that are not overly done. Having a client tell you your work immediately makes them feel right at home is the ultimate compliment.

**WHAT ELEMENT OF STYLE OR PHILOSOPHY DO YOU ADHERE TO WITHOUT FAIL?**

To always listen to clients and always be professional.

**WHAT IS A SINGLE THING YOU'D DO TO BRING A DULL HOUSE TO LIFE?**

Accessorize.

JOHN LASSILA & ASSOCIATES, LTD.
John Lassila, Allied Member ASID
275 Market Street, Suite 299
Minneapolis, MN 55405
612.672.9959
Fax 612.672.9692

# SANDRA MANGEL
## SANDRA MANGEL INTERIOR DESIGN

In partnership with her mother, Eleanor Mady, Sandra Mangel established Two's Company, a retail gift and accessory boutique, in 1974. Thirty years later, the retail aspect of the business was removed, and the space became a showroom for Sandra's interior design work. With the help of her loyal team—project manager Nicole Crow, draftsperson Julie Nordine and design assistant Katie Erickson—she has since forged a name for Sandra Mangel Interiors, Inc., not only in Minnesota but from coast to coast as well.

Sandra attributes her success to her mother's influence. A great lady of style and an accomplished seamstress, Eleanor designed and made her daughter's clothing as well as her own. In so doing, she instilled in her daughter a discerning eye for quality and a love of beautiful fabrics—a characteristic that is apparent in Sandra's keen attention to dressmaker detail in her elegant drapery designs and upholstery treatments.

Along with this inherited talent, Sandra offers her clients the fresh and exciting resources afforded by her extensive travel to major design venues throughout the country and worldwide. Though she hesitates to label her design style—she states that her firm is versatile,

and one could not refer to their work as "cookie cutter" or "one size fits all"—each of her designs reflects classic, timeless style that is comfortable, appropriate and inviting. Her more recent projects include several modern city lofts and condominium spaces in which form, line, texture and the choice of sustainable materials take precedence, new suburban construction in which luxury is paramount and urban remodels in which sensitivity and adherence to architectural integrity prevails.

Sandra directs her focus to her clients' desires from the very outset of a project. She closely listens to their specific needs and wishes and takes cues from their existing environments, lifestyles and personal tastes. Excited about the current trend among

**ABOVE**
Custom-designed cherry and marble fireplace surround and enclose a video center. An iron and glass top cocktail table was custom designed and locally fabricated.
*Photograph by Greg Page*

**FACING PAGE**
Clean lines, warm neutrals, and a rich combination of textures work together to create a serene comfortable and inviting space. The linear lines emphasize the verticality of the architecture of this Lakes of the Isles family room.
*Photograph by Greg Page*

homeowners to remodel rather than relocate, Sandra stays busy creating master suites from adjacent rooms, adding family rooms, renovating and expanding kitchens and converting basements and attics into more usable spaces. These projects are among her favorites, as she loves to work with and reshape space. Her team has the experience and expertise to manage a commission from beginning to end. Regardless of the scope of the project, she remains consistent in her approach and attentiveness.

Sandra figures prominently in the design community, and her outstanding work has been featured in many local and national publications. She has won numerous awards for her commercial and residential projects, including ASID's coveted Designer of Distinction award in 2006, and she served as president of ASID's Minnesota chapter in 2004.

Sandra is inspired by Stendahl's quote, "Beauty is the promise of happiness." She believes that beauty implies order: "It's about attitude and what we are attracted to internally. We seek what is intrinsically good, striving to attain a balance in our lives." It is her distinct privilege to work in a profession that has such a positive effect on people's lives.

**TOP LEFT**
Suited for large-scale entertaining, these two adjoining rooms combine to form this grand style traditional living room. Several seating arrangements distinguish the spaces and also provide for intimate conversation.
*Photograph by Greg Page*

**BOTTOM LEFT**
The Edina kitchen designed for an active family of eight. It features custom-designed maple and cherry cabinets, granite countertops, tumbled marble back splash, an island with twin dish washers, floor-to-ceiling pantries, and a computer desk with ample storage, which is not visible.
*Photograph by Greg Page*

**FACING PAGE LEFT & RIGHT**
The master bath's sconces and chandelier, along with custom-painted and glazed cabinetry, enhance the spa-like elegance. Radiant heated, inlaid marble flooring echoes the mosaic frame and border that surrounds the whirlpool tub.
*Photographs by Greg Page*

# Q&A

## MORE ABOUT SANDRA ...

WHAT COLORS BEST DESCRIBE YOU?

Saturated colors. They are happy and full of energy. Vibrant hues lift my spirit.

WHAT IS THE BEST PART OF BEING AN INTERIOR DESIGNER?

I love that design is never stagnant. When I create, I constantly learn, grow and evolve. But the greatest part of any project is making a difference in my clients' lives by creating environments that exceed their expectations.

IF YOU COULD ELIMINATE ONE DESIGN TECHNIQUE OR STYLE FROM THE WORLD, WHAT WOULD IT BE?

Nothing—all styles and techniques play a part in my personal creative evolution.

WHAT IS THE MOST UNUSUAL DESIGN TECHNIQUE YOU'VE USED IN ONE OF YOUR PROJECTS?

We are in the process of creating Lalique-style custom balustrade panels for a staircase.

SANDRA MANGEL INTERIOR DESIGN
Sandra Mangel, ASID, CID
4601 Bryant Avenue South
Minneapolis, MN 55409
612.827.5395
Fax 612.827.7365
www.sandramangel.com

# SHANNON MARIE

## MORGAN & COMPANY

Inspiration literally means "a drawing in of breath." In ancient times, artists were inspired by the muses, who were believed to literally breathe through song the ideas for artistic creation into the minds of the creators. While we no longer call upon muses for our inspiration, we often do look outside ourselves for that burst of creativity we need. Shannon Marie knows this and has created an entire business around the idea that one's creativity often needs a catalyst.

Shannon began her career in retail merchandising at the age of 15. Over the next decade, she developed her eye for style as a retailer, merchant and buyer on three continents. In her late 20s, she decided she wanted to see more of the world. She helped design a custom-built boat, and she spent the next six years traveling, living in various exotic locales and getting to know a variety of people from all walks of life. Her voyage taught her to make the best use of available space—on a boat it is certainly limited—and exposed her to a variety of regional architectural and design elements.

For Shannon, the inspiration to become an interior designer came upon her return to the States. Her uncle, award-winning photographer William Allard, was visiting her home and

perusing some photographs she had taken of her recent travels and the ship she had helped design. Impressed with her eye for detail, William spoke the sentence that would forever change her professional life: "You could do this for a living." With those words, Shannon's uncle imbued her with the drive she needed to launch her design career.

After earning her degree in interior design from Dakota County Technical College, Shannon opened the doors to Morgan & Company. While her company is small—she has only two employees, one of whom is her mother—she has enjoyed great success. She has done numerous residential projects, and her design and remodeling of the Gillette Children's Hospital, a project she cites as one of the greatest honors of her professional career, was featured in *Architecture Minnesota*.

**ABOVE**
The classic hand-carved gilt mirror and the gold leaf-coved ceiling reflect the light of this guest bath's crystal teardrop chandelier.
*Photograph by Alex Steinberg*

**FACING PAGE**
The sensuous textures of velvet, silk, mohair and linen wash the living room in a natural beauty that reflects the home's majestic setting.
*Photograph by Alex Steinberg*

Shannon designs from the standpoint that homes are places of respite; people go home to ground themselves and rejuvenate. As a designer, she must first discover a client's passions and then build interiors that both reflect and ignite them. She does so through little touches of whimsy—a goldfish in a bowl as a living room centerpiece, for instance—that elicit belly laughs, provoke conversation and invite observation. She infuses a home with life so that it will, in turn, do the same for its residents. Shannon's motto thus rings true: she continually succeeds at "inspiring people to live creative lives."

**ABOVE**
Tom Mosberg's wall sculpture and Shannon's signature table arrangement greet guests as they enter this nature-inspired dining room.
*Photograph by Alex Steinberg*

**FACING PAGE**
For this master bedroom, Morgan & Company blended designs of past, present and future. Marge Carson's Chateau Chaumont bed celebrates the elegance of the French Loire Valley.
*Photograph by Alex Steinberg*

# MORE ABOUT SHANNON ...

**Q&A**

### WHAT IS THE HIGHEST COMPLIMENT YOU'VE RECEIVED PROFESSIONALLY?

At a recent photo shoot of a home I designed, the photographer told me that the house made him feel like he didn't want to leave. Coming from someone who photographs homes for a living, this meant a lot to me.

### WHAT IS A SINGLE THING YOU WOULD DO TO BRING A DULL HOUSE TO LIFE?

Add layers. Bring in something bold, one piece of signature furniture to build from, and then add accessories that give it character—much as a woman would do with the basic black cocktail dress hanging in her closet.

### NAME ONE THING MOST PEOPLE DON'T KNOW ABOUT YOU.

I don't really like to draw attention to myself.

### WHAT COLOR BEST DESCRIBES YOU AND WHY?

I'd have to say white. It's clean and crisp, and there are so many variables because it encompasses the entire spectrum of the rainbow. Like a personality.

### WHAT BOOKS ARE YOU READING RIGHT NOW?

I rarely read only one book at a time. Right now, I'm reading *The Alchemist* by Paulo Coelho and *Sex, Times & Power* by Leonard Shlain.

MORGAN & COMPANY
Shannon Marie
25 North Lake Street, Suite 125
Forest Lake, MN 55025
651.464.1558
Fax 651.464.9438

# MARIE MEKO

## DURR LTD.

A n exceptional life deserves an exceptional home. Marie Meko works with this philosophy in mind.

At once inviting, surprising and inspiring, Marie's designs often reflect the styles of 18th-century Europe. French, English, Scottish and Italian influences merge in her work into an eclectic ancestral style. By reinterpreting classic traditions for contemporary interiors, she creates spaces where past meets present, luxury meets whimsy and elegance meets comfort.

Marie started her career in the designer clothing business, where she acquired her appreciation for color, texture and sumptuous fabrics. While living and working in Santa Monica, California, she honed her design and construction knowledge. When she returned to Minneapolis she joined Durr Ltd., an established design firm.

By creating a close collaboration between architect, designer and client, Marie helps ensure the success of her projects, giving her clients the homes they envision. It is a true source of pride for her and her design team to leave their clients settling into interiors they enjoy and want to share.

Marie's reputation for working on exclusive and historic properties has led to unique projects, including a world-class motor yacht and a hotel and winery in Croatia. For Marie, every project is an exciting opportunity to create a space true to the dreams and lifestyles of her clients. She looks forward to meeting each new challenge and turning ideas into stunning reality.

**ABOVE**
This charming sitting room and kitchen/dining room was once the servant's dining room and screen porch. The banquette was custom made for the room to enjoy the view or watch television, which is housed in an antique trunk. The push of a button lifts the television up for viewing from the two swivel chairs in the foreground. The table in the window is an antique French pastry table with a custom copper top. The corner shelf is antique and displays a collection of Flow Blue dishes. The whimsical pug fabric is Beacon Hill, check drapes from Cowtan and Tout and floral-and-stripe curtains in the dining area are Ralph Lauren. All trays are antique tole.
*Photograph by Alex Steinberg Photography*

**FACING PAGE**
Newly remodeled kitchen of a historic 1920's English Tudor home. Reclaimed beams with plaster and straw between add superb authenticity. Delft tiles decorate the area behind the stove, which has a custom copper hand-hammered hood. The windows and the skirt under sink display Scalamandré Medici Archive fabric. The center island contains a thoughtful collection of antique silver from Europe. Other items include cheese domes under the window and antique Majolica.
*Photograph by Alex Steinberg Photography*

### ABOVE

The beautiful wood paneling from England is original to the home and as such, it was important to reflect the period with custom wing chairs. Fabric is Brunschwig & Fils with a tapestry inset by Old World Weavers. The crewel drapes are Old World Weavers from Stark. Mirrors and cabinets are antique as is the Victorian beaded chair and footstool. Large rooms can present a challenge when doing seating arrangements; a great solution can be a grouping of four chairs around a table that can be used for pleasant conversation and lovely views of the lake and gardens.
*Photograph by Alex Steinberg Photography*

### LEFT

A charming sitting room adjacent to a master bedroom, and a summer sleeping porch. This sunny space is the perfect area to have morning coffee or afternoon tea. Furnishings including a Louis J. Solomon daybed, antique French iron coffee table, embroidered voile fabric attached to antique French corona and an antique tea set complete the feeling. Loveseat and chairs from Hickory House.
*Photograph by Alex Steinberg Photography*

### FACING PAGE

With the addition of antique mirrors, fabric by Old World Weavers and Scalamandré fabric on the existing panels, this remodeled dining room gained new life. The use of two tables in a large dining room provides an intimate space to enjoy dinner with a view of beautiful Lake Superior. The fully upholstered chairs at the end of the table can be drawn closer for versatile seating.
*Photograph by Alex Steinberg Photography*

# MORE ABOUT MARIE ...

## Q&A

WHAT IS THE BEST PART OF BEING AN INTERIOR DESIGNER?

The satisfaction of a client being happy with the result of their project.

WHAT IS THE HIGHEST COMPLIMENT YOU'VE RECEIVED
PROFESSIONALLY?

Repeat business and long-term relationships with clients.

WHAT IS A SINGLE THING YOU WOULD DO TO BRING A DULL HOUSE
TO LIFE?

Add color to the walls.

DURR LTD.
Marie Meko, ASID
810 1st Street South, Suite 130
Hopkins, MN 55343
952.933.3849
Fax 952.933.7719

# LINDA MILLER

## CITIES INTERIORS

Linda Miller, sole owner of Cities Interiors, believes that the success of her firm is attributed to the notion of team, developed throughout her career as an Interior Designer. Linda's definition of team begins with the client, extending to her staff, the architect, contractor and numerous sub-contractors, the marketing group and vendors. Linda understands teamwork must start from a project's conception to custom tailor a beautifully detailed interior that fulfills the clients' aesthetic and functional needs.

Having practiced for 25 years, Linda's passion for interior design extends from single-family residential to loft and condominium development and design. Located in the International Market Square, Cities Interiors is comprised of three senior designers. Cities Interiors has employed designers that bring individual strengths to the table, all having personalities that instinctively understand the others. As lead designer, Linda manages the development of every residence and consults one of the firm's Senior Designers dependant on the stylistic direction of the project. Senior Designer Flora Brama is introduced to the project if a

client desires a Contemporary or Transitional style of design, where a client who prefers a Traditional flavoring is referred to Senior Designer Pam Kilian.

Cities Interiors offers services in Project Management, Space Planning, Interior Architectural Detailing, Finishes and Furnishings. Cities Interiors is proud to have worked with such contractors as Kraus, J.E. Dunn, Dew Corporation, Ryan Construction, Shaw-Lundquist and Architects such as Julie Snow Architects, ESG, Hart Howerton Architects of San Francisco, BKV, HGA, DJR and BTR.

**ABOVE**
Westin St. Paul residence.
*Photograph by Tim Rummelhoff*

**FACING PAGE**
Westin St. Paul residence.
*Photograph by Tim Rummelhoff*

As a company owner and designer to many of the Minneapolis and St. Paul loft and condo developments, Linda takes pride in her part of the "big picture." The firm has developed a reputation for their expertise and experience in their "ground-up abilities," making them distinctively unique from the majority of the Twin Cities Boutique Interior Design firms.

Cities Interiors values timeless design while embracing the future. Cities Interiors is currently pursuing design that employs sustainable products without aesthetic compromise.

**TOP LEFT**
Westin Edina Galleria residence.
*Photograph courtesy of Cities Interiors*

**BOTTOM LEFT**
Westin Edina Galleria residence.
*Photograph courtesy of Cities Interiors*

**FACING PAGE LEFT**
Westin St. Paul residence.
*Photograph by Tim Rummelhoff*

**FACING PAGE RIGHT**
Westin St. Paul residence.
*Photograph by Tim Rummelhoff*

# MORE ABOUT LINDA ...

## Q&A

### DO YOU HAVE A SIGNATURE STYLE?

In the Twin Cities, Traditional design has always been the most common request, but we are seeing an evolution towards Transitional design. As a firm, we are best suited in this area of design. It commingles all of our loves, and our best team effort is reflected in Transitional settings. However, Cities Interiors has a design team of senior designers, each specializing in a different style of design, ranging from Traditional to Contemporary.

### WHAT DOES YOUR FUTURE HOLD?

In the last few years, Cities Interiors has found great success in delivering concept through design time, rather than dealing in a retail furniture market. We believe by providing the client with a vision, we are utilizing our creativity and the client's investment dollars in the most fair and beneficial way. This process enables Cities Interiors to specify products and furnishings that are best suited to the space by way of extending to the client our trade-buying abilities. We are also very focused on all of the exciting developments in Green product design. The product range has become very expansive and continues to grow without compromise in the areas of aesthetics and function.

CITIES INTERIORS
Linda Miller
275 Market Street, Suite 567
Minneapolis, MN 55405
612.337.0084
Fax 612.337.0110

# Lynn Monson
# Sandy Monson

## MONSON INTERIOR DESIGN, INC.

Lynn and Sandy Monson have been working together almost as long as they've been husband and wife. They opened their interior design firm in 1980, two years after they were married.

In the time since, Monson Interior Design has earned a reputation for its high-end kitchen and bath design-build work and has assembled an impressive collection of awards, including numerous state and national awards from the National Kitchen & Bath Association and the American Society of Interior Designers. Through it all, they've kept their company small, working together but alone in their Minneapolis studio and on projects throughout the Twin Cities metro area and beyond.

Sure, they've had plenty of opportunities to expand. But, Lynn says, that waters down your purpose and limits your ability to give even the tiniest detail your utmost attention—and one thing the designers take great pride in is their hands-on approach to every job. And because Lynn is a licensed contractor, in addition to their both being licensed designers, Monson is able to offer total turnkey projects.

They are also proud of the fact that they lack a signature style. Instead, they say, they surrender their personal preferences and design to the architecture of the space, the tastes of the clients and a collaborative vision. And clients who trust that approach—like the homeowner for whom Lynn and Sandy built a kitchen in a warren of rooms that had once been back-of-the-house servant quarters or the gentleman who presented the designers with a load of imported amber glass block and asked them to incorporate it somehow—are the most fun to work with.

**ABOVE**
A contemporary log cabin guest bath combines traditional Norwegian roots with a Japanese aesthetic. Cherry, teak, cedar and slate contrast with mirror, glass and chrome.
*Photograph by Jim Brandenburg*

**FACING PAGE**
The three-part island of geometric shapes in a mix of materials is the focal point of this contemporary kitchen. Red accents provide an exclamation point.
*Photograph by Trends Publishing International, photographer Tim Maloney*

Because their designs are one-of-a-kind treatments, Lynn and Sandy are often called upon to think outside the box and go to great lengths to give every client something special. One couple, Sandy recalls, wanted their very kitchen to be sculptural art. Incorporating five cabinet woods and four countertop materials at varying heights, the result was a striking display of six distinct stations in varied shapes and colors and of various materials, defining the kitchen functions while providing interplay of textures.

And though that might sound complicated, it is, like all of Lynn and Sandy's work, simply stunning.

**TOP LEFT**
Old and new is artfully combined in this Italian kitchen. Traditional stone carvings and a wood-burning oven coexist with stainless steel appliances and Euro-modern cabinetry.
*Photograph by Dana Wheelock*

**BOTTOM LEFT**
The striking textural combination of granite, maple, cherry and copper comes to life in the abundant natural light of the two-story kitchen addition.
*Photograph by Karen Melvin*

**FACING PAGE**
Kitchen cabinetry embellishments—mouldings, spindles, corbels—are details worthy of the elegant 1910 home. Upper cabinets fronted with stained-glass doors are lit from within.
*Photograph by Dana Wheelock*

# MORE ABOUT LYNN & SANDY ...

Q&A

**LYNN, WHAT SINGLE THING WOULD YOU DO TO BRING A DULL HOUSE TO LIFE?**

Improve the lighting (including natural light) by adding more lighting, better types of lighting and more lighting controls. Light is one of the most powerful things that affect how a person feels about a space.

**SANDY, IF YOU COULD ELIMINATE ONE DESIGN/ARCHITECTURAL/ BUILDING TECHNIQUE OR STYLE FROM THE WORLD, WHAT WOULD IT BE?**

As my "edit, simplify, refine" philosophy suggests, I don't much care for an excess of detail, preferring instead clean lines and uncluttered spaces. Frou-frou blocks the chakras.

**WHAT ONE ELEMENT OF STYLE OR PHILOSOPHY HAVE YOU STUCK WITH FOR YEARS THAT STILL WORKS FOR YOU TODAY?**

Sandy: Edit. Simplify. Refine.

Lynn: Especially in the kitchen and bath, everything has to function well. If it doesn't work, it doesn't matter how great it looks.

**WHAT DO YOU LIKE MOST ABOUT DOING BUSINESS IN MINNEAPOLIS?**

Inspiration is never far away. The city is home to a thriving arts community that is supported both privately and publicly: Live theater, art and history museums and world-class architecture are just a few examples of the area's cultural offerings.

MONSON INTERIOR DESIGN
Lynn Monson, ASID, CID, CKD, CBD
Sandy Monson, ASID, CID
1221 Cedar Lake Road South
Minneapolis, MN 55416
612.338.0665

# JAMES NOBLE

## NOBLE INTERIORS INC.

I f communication is key to interior design success who better to facilitate this vital client-centered relationship than an interior design veteran who just happens to be the father of five. As James Noble expounds, you certainly must have communication skills and patience to conquer both vocations successfully, which he has for the past 33 years, just ask his legions of loyal clients and his wife of 23 years.

In his three decades in the business, James has pioneered many firsts, one of which was the opening of the first Holly Hunt Showroom in Minneapolis, which was her first showroom out of the Chicago area. He has also owned his own retail store and today he runs his own design practice, Noble Interiors Inc.

During initial client meetings, as with the theme threaded throughout his life, he encourages mutual communication. As a husband and father, Jim has learned to listen first and ask questions second. After garnering all the information, he develops a design program based on his clients' individual needs and lifestyle. His design format is an accumulation of knowledge of the design discipline coupled with his extensive knowledge of the furniture world and most importantly, all of his experience orchestrated into the perfect design for his clients.

**LEFT**
"The Little French Church," commissioned painting of St. Louis, King of France, hangs in this opulent dining room.
*Photograph by Landmark Photography*

A full-service design firm, Noble Interiors Inc. guides each client from a space plan through installation. Jim's ultimate goal is to improve the client's comfort at home or at work. With each project, he is not only gratified by his client's satisfaction and joy but is pleased to have shared his talent—as in the case of a client who once told him, "Although I didn't even know what I wanted, I received exactly what I could not express."

Classically trained, Jim admittedly loves both Traditional and Contemporary designs; however, Contemporary styles must be timeless. Not one to follow trends, he designs with color and comfort and all of those elements that withstand the test of time. Thus, Jim is known for his classic designs no matter the desired style.

His work can be seen all over Minnesota and even in the Governor's Mansion. Jim believes good design work is rewarded, and his reward is that he continues to do what he loves every day.

**ABOVE**
Custom tiles were painted in France for this condominium kitchen remodel.
*Photograph by Landmark Photography*

**FACING PAGE**
The bathroom features impressionistic paintings, new millwork with a hand-rubbed finish and a custom vanity.
*Photograph by Landmark Photography*

# Q&A

## MORE ABOUT JAMES ...

WHAT IS THE HIGHEST COMPLIMENT YOU'VE RECEIVED PROFESSIONALLY?

A recent client stated, "Jim has the most impeccable vision and exquisite taste. Plus, he's fun."

NAME ONE THING THAT MOST PEOPLE DON'T KNOW ABOUT YOU.

As a very involved parent, I love rolling up my sleeves and working at my children's school, in addition to attending their various events.

WHAT PHILOSOPHY HAVE YOU STUCK WITH FOR YEARS THAT STILL WORKS FOR YOU TODAY?

I follow what I call the four C's of great design—character, comfort, color and continuity.

WHO HAS HAD THE BIGGEST INFLUENCE ON YOUR CAREER?

My career has been influenced by many, but in particular Mark Hampton, John Fowler and Holly Hunt.

NOBLE INTERIORS INC.
James Noble, Allied Member ASID, CKBR, NARI
Minneapolis, MN
612.904.0933
www.nobleinteriorsinc.com

# MARTHA O'HARA

## MARTHA O'HARA INTERIORS

M artha O'Hara and her talented designers approach each project as a creative team, which allows their clients the ultimate expression of dynamic design solutions. Above all, their goal is to give their clients the "confidence to express themselves in bolder and more distinct ways" than they might achieve on their own. From initial discussion and concept, through design and installation, Martha O'Hara Interiors handles every step in the process, making each project an enjoyable and rewarding experience.

Martha believes that her studio is exceptional, especially for its integral team approach. Though there will always be a lead designer directing any project, it is the contribution and exponential vision of the team of 10 that produces stunning design. Working closely with the client, the lead designer develops the broad creative vision and direction of the job. The team then delves into the details, choosing furnishings that are most appropriate to the personal style of the client. By approaching each project from the client's vantage point, the designers at Martha O'Hara Interiors give their clients what they've always wanted but just needed the "expert eyes" to achieve. That professional guidance takes them beyond their initial ideas and vision to the camera-ready abundant creativity and solid design now unfolded in their home.

**LEFT**
"Luxury by the Lake"—Champagne neutrals are accented with rich persimmon paisley and sumptuous pear velvet in an elegant yet approachable great room.
*Photograph by Greg Page of Page Studios Inc.*

The firm's projects are comprised primarily of residential and a few smaller commercial commissions. One such ongoing project is in conjunction with The LUSSO Collection, which owns an exclusive resort group of luxury properties throughout the world. O'Hara Interiors is responsible for the interior designs and furnishings for many of these spacious and exquisite properties. Although this assignment might sound daunting to other design firms, Martha approaches the illustrious project as she does every other project—whether expansive or diminutive— with enthusiasm and passion.

**ABOVE**
Light adds depth to the vibrant metal sculpture on the far wall, while bright orange accents spice up dark mahogany woods and textural neutrals in the great room of a LUSSO Collection resort home.
*Photograph by Richard Springgate*

**RIGHT**
Aggregate walls, mullioned glass planes and cedar ceilings infuse a Bauhaus loft office with contemporary charm.
*Photograph by Richard Springgate*

**FACING PAGE**
Sinuous curves and sleek surfaces abound in this contemporary kitchen.
*Photograph by Richard Springgate*

It is the relational side of the business that Martha enjoys most. Working with scores of appreciative families makes everything she does worth every ounce of her time and effort. Her strength lies in the front-end space planning of each project where she gains a feel for what the particular family needs. A beautiful interior is hardly practical if it is not tailored to that family's lifestyle or needs, and Martha knows interiors are spectacular in their entirety when they are both pleasing and functional. Martha believes that her true strength is leading and inspiring her team of talented designers to create those spectacular interiors.

Martha O'Hara Interiors takes a project from concept to completion to the very last detail. While some designers are working on the next project before the last one is completely installed, Martha's team is still following up on the delivery service, arranging the accessories in the bookshelves and locating that beautiful final centerpiece for the table that often concludes their labors of love and professional commitment.

The firm has amassed a complete and diverse portfolio that meets the needs of their clients. Judging by the fact that most of Martha's business is repeat and referral, she can be assured her clients feel they have been treated to professionally complete and unique service as well.

**ABOVE**
Deep earth tones and highly tactile fabrics provide a grounding effect and transform this bright and airy La Jolla beach home into a cozy place to kick back after a day in the surf.
*Photograph by Richard Springgate*

**FACING PAGE**
This serene master suite includes a tufted leather bed, comfortable sitting area and sleek rattan chaise. The light of an outdoor table lamp beckons guests to relax and enjoy ocean breezes on the adjoining patio.
*Photograph by Richard Springgate*

# MORE ABOUT MARTHA ...

**Q&A**

**WHAT PROJECT ARE YOU MOST PROUD OF?**

There are two projects that compete for the top spot. One of my favorite projects was a home that we did a year ago in Idaho. We had an existing home that was totally renovated and remodeled with a big addition on the back. The clients had allowed us to quarterback the entire remodel and then passed the whole home over to us to furnish. The large glass conservatory that rests on a 30-foot peninsula on a mountain lake is one of the most stunning rooms our team has ever furnished.

The other project is a LUSSO luxury property set near the ocean in La Jolla, California. The architecture of the home is inspired by the work done in the 1920s by Rudolph Schindler, a protégé and colleague of Frank Lloyd Wright. The home is a highly functional and equally stunning blend of stone, concrete, cedar, steel and glass.

Furnishing its interior was especially delightful for our team, since LUSSO allowed us to stretch our imaginations and creative abilities when choosing items worthy of the space.

**WHAT IS THE GREATEST LESSON YOU'VE LEARNED?**

When I started my interior design business, I was aware of certain skills that I possessed but I wondered if I could make them marketable. What I have learned since is that if you are proud of your designs, then you can sell them. Most clients recognize good design and buy good design. I think that selling ability was something that I learned and developed over time. I always tell my designers that you need to like your clients, really get into the projects, do strong design for them and then the selling will take care of itself.

MARTHA O'HARA INTERIORS
Martha O'Hara
8353 Excelsior Boulevard
Hopkins, MN 55343
952.908.3150
Fax 952.908.3153
www.oharainteriors.com

# GIGI OLIVE
## GIGI OLIVE INTERIORS, LLC

Gigi Olive Interiors, LLC was founded in 1999 to produce spectacular interiors that are intended to reflect the personality and goals of the individual who resides within these majestic interior landscapes.

Through a combination of good listening, design know-how and more than 20 years of experience, Gigi Olive creates specific designs for individual clients that cater to their needs, dreams and desires. She knows that a successful project is more than an exquisite design; it involves building relationships with each client that last for years and through multiple dwellings.

Working high-end residential projects, Gigi's services include project management, new construction, remodeling or redesigning of an existing space with a flair for comfort, style and functionality.

Feng Shui is an important design philosophy to Gigi. This 5,000-year-old "Chinese art of placement" philosophy can improve one's health, wealth and happiness. Meaning "wind and water," Feng Shui concentrates on the flow of energy and movement within a space, which leaves clients feeling comfortable and relaxed within their interior spaces.

Another valuable aspect of Gigi's services is her dedication to producing designs that are environmentally friendly. There is a growing concern with conservation issues in today's world. Gigi strives to reuse as many resources as possible in her projects by recycling, using reclaimed materials and being aware of the materials' origin.

No matter the size or scope of a project, Gigi applies her expertise and experience to create a space that reflects the tastes and needs of her clients and upon completion always differentiates between a house to live in and an inviting, beautiful, distinctive home.

**ABOVE**
In this early 1900's house converted to a condominium, the antique Asian table and Brazilian chest add an element of ethnic interest and contrast to this calm retreat.
*Photograph by Karen Melvin*

**FACING PAGE**
This grand living room captures the elegance of many fine fabrics and classic furnishings while "Madame X" reigns above.
*Photograph by Chuck Carver*

GIGI OLIVE INTERIORS, LLC
Gigi Olive, ASID, CID
275 Market Street
Minneapolis, MN 55405
612.341.4020
Fax 612.341.4026
www.gigioliveinteriors.com

# LISA PECK
# KRISTEN MENGELKOCH
### PISA DESIGN, INC.

Interior designers Lisa Peck and Kristen Mengelkoch are experts at translating their clients' unique needs and stylistic preferences into beautiful, functional spaces that nurture each resident's personal aspirations.

The clientele of Minneapolis-based Pisa Design, Inc. is as diverse as its designers' capabilities. From Traditional Victorian to cutting-edge Contemporary or a transitional mixture of the two, Lisa and Kristen have the talent to exceed even the most discerning patrons' dreams. The principals pride themselves on their ability to adapt to any situation and relate to young parents, singles, combined families and empty-nesters alike. One family's quality of life was tremendously improved with the thoughtful design of a mudroom; each child had a special place for their outerwear and an inbox for homework assignments, and parents were treated to harmonious comings and goings.

New construction or renovation, large project or one-room remodel, Lisa and Kristen flourish in challenging situations, such as finding common ground among clients with

seemingly opposing predilections for style. The principals believe that the key to a successful design is listening intently to create breathtaking spaces that complement the residents' goals and interests. Some clients desire minimal upkeep to allow for more recreation time; others need home offices, professional-grade kitchens, hobby rooms, teenager-friendly hangouts or elaborate entertaining spaces. Each Pisa creation is delightful, fresh and matches the client's lifestyle, style and even sense of humor.

To make certain that everyone from client to contractors can envision the final result and have an accurate idea of the project expenditure, the designers prepare detailed construction

**ABOVE**
A Victorian bath remodel maximizes space and adds cheery, warm color. Metal panel hides the radiator.
*Photograph by Alex Steinberg Photography*

**FACING PAGE**
This cozy bar is newly constructed, but its heirloom-quality detailing and finishes create a look of generations past.
*Photograph by Alex Steinberg Photography*

documentation as needed: floor plans, elevations and sections, demolition plans, furniture plans, lighting plans, millwork and tile details, and written finish and fixture specifications.

Whether on vacation, working with clients or going about their daily lives, Lisa and Kristen are constantly absorbing design ideas and pondering the residential interior applicability of each. They savor a book's vivid descriptions of place, regional architectural conventions such as covered entrances in Arizona or Italy's earthen building materials, unique color combinations of saltwater fish and interesting textures of Native American beadwork. While the partners work independently on projects, clients have the benefit of a team of designers—and their unique experiences and perspectives—collaborating on their behalf.

Pisa Design, Inc. was established in 1995 on the foundation of Lisa and Kristen's interior design bachelor's degrees, many years spent honing their skills with other firms and a shared passion for creative expression. The firm has received numerous ASID Minnesota awards, including Best of Residential Design, and has been featured by several regional periodicals, yet the greatest recognition comes from clients who wholeheartedly express how greatly the introspective design has enriched their lives.

**TOP LEFT**
The remodeled kitchen features a sophisticated mix of zebra wood, maple, stainless steel, granite and back-painted glass tile. Curved metal brackets support the rounded peninsula.
*Photograph by Mark A. Kawell Photography*

**BOTTOM LEFT**
Traditional touches warm the edges of this contemporary formal entertaining space. A panel of fish fossils hangs above the fireplace.
*Photograph by Mark A. Kawell Photography*

**FACING PAGE LEFT**
Sleek granite contrasts with two kinds of limestone that flow in from the home's exterior. The smoked glass sink is lit from below.
*Photograph by Mark A. Kawell Photography*

**FACING PAGE RIGHT**
Green flooring emphasizes the relationship between inside and outside. Cabinet and millwork finish placement continues the interplay between horizontal and vertical planes.
*Photograph by Mark A. Kawell Photography*

# MORE ABOUT LISA & KRISTEN ...

**HOW DO YOU INJECT THE DESIGN PROCESS WITH FUN?**

We foster an environment where people can freely express their wishes, concerns, preferences and needs. We make the design process enjoyable by putting everyone at ease and showing our clients that we care.

**KRISTEN, HOW DID YOU DECIDE TO PURSUE THIS PROFESSION?**

Just as I was completing my business baccalaureate, a friend showed me presentation boards for his interior design class. The idea became more and more appealing, until I finally went back to school to follow my true passion.

**LISA, WHAT IS THE HIGHEST COMPLIMENT THAT YOU HAVE RECEIVED?**

Someone asked a client of mine for a list of interior designer referrals and he told me, "You weren't part of the list, you are the list."

PISA DESIGN, INC.
Lisa Peck, ASID
Kristen Mengelkoch, Allied Member ASID
4500 Park Glen Road, Suite 260
Minneapolis, MN 55416
952.926.3572
www.pisadesigninc.com

# MARK PETERSON
## M|A|PETERSON DESIGNBUILD, INC.

**M**|A|Peterson Designbuild, Inc. is an interdisciplinary design-build firm that transcends the boundaries of design and construction; many clients find these services convenient, inspiring and simply irresistible.

With an all encompassing and holistic approach, Mark Peterson works with his clients from blueprints to construction through interior design and furnishings, even landscaping. Each client receives a customized package of services based entirely on what they need to create their ideal home, inside and out.

Although their work is primarily remodels, Mark's firm does build new high-end residential projects as well. With designers, architects, project managers and an experienced support staff, they offer services that include architectural design, construction, interior design, landscape design, landscape production and almost anything in between. They even design and manufacture custom cabinetry and millwork for each client in their own shop. Every design or construction-related issue can be resolved by Mark's highly dynamic team.

One of the hallmarks of M|A|Peterson is that every project they lend their skilled hands to is aesthetically different; they strive to create specific design solutions based upon each client's needs and desires. Most of their work can be classified as Traditional or Classical in nature and has been described as Cutting-Edge Traditional, which Mark says "is a fresh restatement of traditional elements within today's lifestyle."

**LEFT**
With a high sense of style, this front entry welcomes visitors with a marble floor medallion, reconditioned crystal light fixtures, dramatic art and a small glimpse of connected spaces.
*Photograph by Tim Maloney*

When his clients' friends and families visit Mark's redesigned homes they often remark that they feel the homes have life, soul and that the designs posses the character and personality of that particular homeowner. He strives to create a statement of each client's personality seamlessly translated into their home through a timeless solution.

With a multi-step design-build process, Mark feels he gives his clients a comprehensive product from beginning to end. From the early phases when all possibilities are considered through to the quality completion of the project to the walk-through review of the home 11 months later, everything the company does is intended to ensure quality communication and complete client satisfaction.

The people and the processes established by Mark and company truly sets them apart from their competition because very few businesses effectively deliver this wide a variety of services under one roof. These bundled services, integrated as one, provide clients with greater efficiencies, better design, and ultimately a better home and a more enjoyable experience.

**TOP LEFT**
Smooth textures, earthy materials and a soothing palette of color create a relaxing lower-level living space for today's busy family.
*Photograph by Tim Maloney*

**BOTTOM LEFT**
With a fresh, classic feel that ideally suits a large family, this dramatic kitchen retains its connection with the past and appropriateness within the home.
*Photograph by Tim Maloney*

**FACING PAGE LEFT**
Delicate application of traditional Eastern design fundamentals turned a small, cramped kitchen into an open and free-flowing space without adding square footage.
*Photograph by Tim Maloney*

**FACING PAGE RIGHT**
A cabinet wall of dark stained walnut with custom door style and wood-barreled arch interplays with the light fixtures, hardware and wall color to create a rich elegance beyond that of a typical owners suite closet.
*Photograph by Tim Maloney*

# MORE ABOUT MARK ...

**WHAT DO YOU LIKE MOST ABOUT DOING BUSINESS IN YOUR LOCALE?**

The diversity of home styles and variety of distinctive neighborhoods in our area are wonderful. There are so many authentic homes that people value and want to preserve and improve. It provides a wonderful baseline for our business. But really it's the people here that make this a great job. The clients we work with are all very down-to-Earth and appreciative; they're wonderful people who deserve everything we can give them.

**WHAT IS THE BEST PART OF BEING A DESIGNER?**

The best part of design-build is the ability to create a home that perfectly suits each individual family. Working together with our clients, we can re-work or create a new living space that not only is well built and beautiful, but allows them to live each and every day exactly as they would like. The result is a house that is as unique as the family that calls it home.

MIA|PETERSON DESIGNBUILD, INC.
Mark Peterson
6161 Wooddale Avenue
Edina, MN 55424
952.925.9455
Fax 952.925.0644
www.mapeterson.com

# KIM SALMELA

KIM SALMELA

Recently bidding adieu—for now—to one phase of her very illustrious and wildly fulfilling career, designer Kim Salmela is embarking on what she feels is the second phase of her career: A truly focused return to product design (she had her own furniture line for three years in Los Angeles and sold to other retailers such as Neiman Marcus and Horchow) and an expansion into commercial design. Her dream jobs include individually owned funky restaurants and boutique hotels where the design is viewed as being critical to the success of the establishment.

A seasoned entrepreneur and designer for the past 12 years, Kim has owned a succession of home furnishings and lifestyle shops including Paris Flea Market, Belle Époque and most recently, one of Minneapolis' favorite design resources, Alfred's Grand Petit Magasin. This 15,000-square-foot mini department store had been a favorite for numerous clients who appreciated its true originality as well as its charming café. As unique as its moniker, the store was named in honor of a painting Kim found in the south of France and just couldn't resist. It depicts a captivating poodle named simply, Alfred.

Even while some recent college graduates might flounder, Kim knew exactly what she wanted to do with her time and talents: lifestyle enhancement. Before heeding her inner

entrepreneurial calling and going on to own and operate several other businesses, Kim worked for the singer Prince and his company Paisley Park.

Known for her design "guts" and amazing flair for European-infused design, Kim strives for fashionably livable spaces inspired by her very unique and distinctive eye. She attributes her style to extensive travel, her biggest inspiration. Having studied in Milan, Italy—where she purposely avoided a formal education in interior design so that she could instead develop her own diverse tastes and talents rather than an emulation of someone else's—Kim took advantage of her location to explore Europe at every chance. Those experiences still call to her and she has returned many times to shop for antiques, work and seek inspiration. She even had the rare opportunity to decorate an amazing 11th-century French castle, custom-designing every piece of upholstery there, including sofas that had to fit up a 24-inch-wide winding staircase.

**ABOVE**
Kim added warmth and pizzazz to this small powder room by using a bold decorative paint finish.
*Photograph by Edward Bock*

**FACING PAGE**
The stacked stone and Venetian plaster fireplace with stainless steel frame was designed to contrast the wood paneled walls in this retro-modern living room.
*Photograph by Edward Bock*

The greatest elements of her foreign influence are weaved throughout everything Kim designs, from her clients' rooms to her furniture to the one-of-a-kind accessories she always made sure to offer in her stores. To Kim, there is always an emphasis on luxury and the notion that aesthetic beauty is not superficial. Beauty, in whatever form, improves our lives and makes us feel at peace and comforted.

Her staunch goal is to create unique custom interiors that satisfy clients' needs while reflecting their personalities and tastes through an inspiring attention to detail. And as a native of the Twin Cities, Kim has followed as the design of the quietly metropolitan Twin Cities has grown and evolved from Traditional to Contemporary to a lovely fusion of both in Transitional. By mixing perfectly selected accessories and furniture with bold elements or with pieces her clients already own, but never realized quite how to showcase, Kim uncovers the most personalized look for each client. From clients who require a slight home makeover to clients with bare walls, Kim takes on her projects with the same enthusiasm she began with when she opened the doors to her first entrepreneurial venture at the tender age of 23.

Kim Salmela is proving that if "you can dream it, it can be" both with her own design career and in the design spaces of her clients.

**TOP LEFT**
Kim created an eclectic, traditional look by starting with the homeowners' 12'x25' family heirloom rug and then added a piece at a time, such as the antique chairs from France.
*Photograph by Edward Bock*

**BOTTOM LEFT**
"Black!" was this teen's color of choice, so Kim compromised by adding aqua walls and red accents. The blackout shades are hand-painted by Kim as a cost-saving solution for the windows.
*Photograph by Edward Bock*

**FACING PAGE**
The two large, gold-gilt antique chairs, reupholstered in shades of purple velvet, are the foundation of this eclectic room set against an all cream backdrop.
*Photograph by Edward Bock*

# MORE ABOUT KIM...

### Q&A

**WHO HAS HAD THE BIGGEST INFLUENCE ON YOUR CAREER?**

Probably my parents. Both of them equally, because my mom is whacky and creative and my father is a little more pragmatic. My parents also value design and aesthetics and that was passed on to me.

**WHAT IS A SINGLE THING THAT YOU WOULD DO TO A DULL HOUSE TO BRING IT TO LIFE?**

Color the walls. Paint is the least expensive way to completely change the look of a room.

**WHAT SEPARATES YOU FROM YOUR COMPETITION?**

I have a completely different eye than anyone else in the ability to combine old and new. You will not walk into one of my rooms and have it be 100 percent Barbra Barry or 100 percent Baker. I like to mix styles and I can make a room that is classic by mixing many different eras. Even if I'm working in a style that is more Modern, I will still mix in something that is 100 years old because I really think that is the design of today: Being able to mix periods and styles flawlessly.

KIM SALMELA
Kim Salmela
Minneapolis, MN
612.840.5580
www.kimsalmela.com

# KATIE SIDENBERG
## ROBERT SIDENBERG INTERIOR DESIGN

For Katie Sidenberg of Robert Sidenberg Interior Design, extraordinary interior design is a family tradition that she continues with an immense sense of pride. "My father was a very respected interior designer in Minneapolis for 50 years," Katie said. In 1973 she offered to temporarily help her father within his design studio and as it turned out, she never left.

Robert was trained in London and Paris as an artist, and in turn he taught his daughter many valuable lessons in aesthetics. He taught her a great sense of style and a wonderful eye for color, which she implements on a daily basis with her own designs. Through his appreciation for art, history and style, Katie has garnered a unique sense of originality—she never follows trends.

In a nutshell, she calls her style classic, stylish and comfortable, always with an emphasis on wonderful colors. When approaching a new project, she usually wants to change everything from the furniture to the wall colors by updating the style. Clients say that Katie is very easy to work with, that she is fun and that she has a genius eye for color.

Defying the current trend of under-decorated, monochromatic interior designs, Katie always blazes new trails with each project. She does this by mixing different styles,

to achieve a very relaxed, elegant look and feel, much to her clients' satisfaction. For Katie, the most fulfilling aspect of her career as an interior designer is meeting new clients and being able to change their lives by making their environment a more beautiful place in which to live. She does this by providing a very personalized service, being very original and making each project's design process enjoyable.

A classically trained designer, Katie always tries to have fun with her projects and via color or antique pieces add her own style to create a rare interior environment. She always tries to add whimsy that makes her interiors more original and inspiring.

In the future, Katie will continue to create wonderfully comfortable and pleasing interiors that will inspire her clients and enhance their lives.

**ABOVE**
Soft yellow, greens and blues make for a calming and cozy living room.
*Photograph by Richard Leo Johnson*

**FACING PAGE**
A fresh, inviting foyer draws one into this charming home.
*Photograph by Richard Leo Johnson*

# Q&A

## MORE ABOUT KATIE ...

**WHAT PERSONAL INDULGENCES DO YOU SPEND THE MOST MONEY ON?**

My dogs and cowboy boots.

**WHAT COLOR BEST DESCRIBES YOU?**

Green, because I have a very chameleon-like personality.

**YOU CAN TELL I LIVE IN THIS LOCALE BECAUSE ...**

I have 15 winter coats and 25 cashmere sweaters.

**WHAT IS THE HIGHEST COMPLIMENT YOU'VE RECEIVED PROFESSIONALLY?**

That I have an amazing eye for color and that my designs are so comfortable.

ROBERT SIDENBERG INTERIOR DESIGN
Katie Sidenberg, Allied Member ASID
275 Market Street, Suite 546
Minneapolis, MN 55405
612.339.6660
Fax 612.339.5431
www.robertsidenberg.com

**TOP RIGHT**
This space features a colorful, eclectic mix of crisp patterns combined with family heirlooms.
*Photograph by Alex Steinberg*

**BOTTOM RIGHT**
A colorfully vibrant and happy kitchen eating area offers a new take on the Old West.
*Photograph by Susan Gilmore*

**FACING PAGE**
This sunroom features textural and classic elements for reading and relaxing.
*Photograph by Susan Gilmore*

# GREG WALSH
## WALSH DESIGN GROUP

Founded in 1994 by Greg Walsh, Walsh Design Group creates interior designs for clients that desire exceptional design work, encompassing styles from Contemporary, Transitional to European Traditional.

After earning his degree at the University of Wisconsin-Stout, Greg was ready to apply his enthusiasm, knowledge and talent into his chosen vocation. Today with 17 years of experience in the field, Greg has fine-tuned his specialization to include interior architectural detailing and designing. The primary goal for his firm is design that works functionally as well as aesthetically.

A full-service design firm, which addresses both new construction and remodeling projects, Walsh Design Group works seamlessly with individual clients and a variety of distinguished builders and architects. Specializing in unique cabinetry design, interior and exterior architectural details and finishes, Greg's team of 11 completes floor-to-ceiling design. Each in-house designer brings a wealth of experience, strength and value to the firm and its

clients. Working within architectural elements always infinitely helps the end product as the designers have purposely modeled and manipulated the details with a bigger picture in mind.

Along with the firm's interior architectural detailing strength, the design team also excels at the elements that make a house a home. From furniture, textiles, accessories and art, they have developed an extensive collection of resources from across the country and around the world, allowing them to make each project a beautiful and unique reflection of their client's personal style.

**ABOVE**
Faux bois paneled walls, ornamental iron railing and leaded glass clear story windows welcome guests to this entry.
*Photograph by Alex Steinberg*

**FACING PAGE**
Hand-hewn beams, paired chandeliers, and rich textured upholstery envelope this Old World library.
*Photograph by Alex Steinberg*

**TOP LEFT**
Thick, luxurious fabrics, coupled with mixed materials provide a very inviting atmosphere for this homeowner.
*Photograph by Alex Steinberg*

**BOTTOM LEFT**
The faux-finished island highlights the stained cabinetry in this spacious Irish Country-inspired kitchen.
*Photograph by Alex Steinberg*

**FACING PAGE TOP**
Elegance meets Contemporary through this 1950's remodel within this finely appointed home. Visual interest was created by combining comfortable textures, lighting and classic lines.
*Photograph by John Christenson*

**FACING PAGE BOTTOM**
The combination of vertical and horizontal lines throughout the dining room gives an air of urban sophistication.
*Photograph by John Christenson*

Many clients are often unsure of what design styles work for their home and lifestyle, or even where to begin. Greg realizes that uncertainty is remedied through open client communication. The team thoroughly guides their clients through the entire process, gleaning their tastes, lifestyle and inspirations through these design meetings. They also conduct a color analysis that offers the designers insight on clients' color preferences. Many clients are pleasantly surprised at the close personal interest Greg and his team take in their homes and find they are put at ease; as a result, the design process runs flawlessly with no surprises.

Scale, proportion and detail are always critical to Greg on every project: he comments that if he had a signature look it would be the attention to these details. It is little wonder that he spends a great deal of time educating his clients as to how those elements can enhance a project's outcome. "Many people

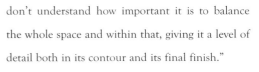

don't understand how important it is to balance the whole space and within that, giving it a level of detail both in its contour and its final finish."

Never one to be complacent in business or in life, six years ago, Greg opened his retail home furnishings store aptly named ID Inside Design, which is centered on modern living. It has been a lovely avenue for a soft entry into the design world for many of his customers as the store carries a variety of furniture, accessories and other soft goods that tend to jump-start a project.

From the blueprint stage to the final pillow placed, Walsh Design Group assists its clients in achieving what they had always hoped was possible.

**TOP LEFT**
Conveying warmth, character and whimsy, this lower level pub area is a unique blend of warm wood tones, patina copper countertops and stone walls.
*Photograph by Alex Steinberg*

**BOTTOM LEFT**
Large birch beams evoke a warm today feel with a sophisticated mix of textures and color. The stone fireplace creates a warm and inviting area, perfect for a long conversation.
*Photograph by Alex Steinberg*

**FACING PAGE LEFT**
Bold architecture details, custom millwork and refined finishes define the classic estate.
*Photograph by Alex Steinberg*

**FACING PAGE RIGHT**
The mansard ceiling, custom cabinetry and classic appointments set the stage for this great room.
*Photograph by Alex Steinberg*

# MORE ABOUT GREG ...

## Q&A

WHAT SINGLE THING WOULD YOU DO TO BRING A DULL HOUSE TO LIFE?

Typically if you have one opportunity, try color.

IF YOU COULD ELIMINATE ONE ARCHITECTURAL STYLE FROM THE WORLD WHAT WOULD IT BE AND WHY?

Victorian—it's fussy and it is very delicate. The extensive use of patterns and color render it formal, leaving it feeling unlivable.

WHO OR WHAT HAS HAD THE BIGGEST INFLUENCE ON YOUR CAREER?

Stylistically, what we do is so broad there is not just one driving force or entity that I feel has steered us in one direction or has influenced us. I believe our clients are our single most influential drive.

**WALSH DESIGN GROUP**
Greg Walsh, Allied Member ASID, BATC, NARI
211 North First Street
Minneapolis, MN 55401
612.317.0045
Fax 612.317.0046
www.walshdesigngroup.com

# LOLA WATSON

## LOLA WATSON INTERIOR DESIGN, LLC

Designer Lola Watson brings a unique perspective to her work. Along with her training and background in interior design, Lola is also a professional opera singer. She credits the discipline of opera with reinforcing the fundamentals of good design, which are balance and form.

An award-winning, nationally published interior designer, Lola began her career in the design studio of Rich's Department Store in Atlanta and then moved to Minneapolis where she was a designer with downtown Dayton's Interior Design Studio and then Gabbert's Design Studio. Years later, in Minneapolis, she resumed her interior design career at Gabbert's and then as a senior designer with William Beson Interior Design Studio, ultimately opening her own business in International Market Square in 2003. In between, Lola sang for a number of years with the San Francisco Opera company, an exciting time that took her around the world and exposed her to many different cultures and lifestyles.

When she returned, she brought her expanded sense of aesthetics with her to Minneapolis and to her new clients. "I realized that the world was full of options," she says. "It would have been a shame not to use those many varied choices to benefit my clients."

For Lola, her work—and her reward—are all about creating aesthetically pleasing homes that are functional havens where clients can refresh their spirits. Along with client satisfaction—her main objective—she likes to help them raise their own aesthetic awareness. "Even the most mundane item or task can have an inherent beauty, if it's well and thoughtfully designed," says Lola. "Just because something is functional doesn't mean its form can't be beautiful."

**ABOVE**
Watson restored the living room of the historic Palmer House of Rochester to its former English manor house grandeur during a Designer's Showcase.
*Photograph by Karen Melvin*

**FACING PAGE**
Luxurious fabrics and a theatrical drapery treatment balances a Steinway Grand and sets the stage for an elegant music room in this Edina townhome of a local recording artist.
*Photograph by Karen Melvin*

**ABOVE**
This Lake Mooney home was inspired by Scottish designer and architect Charles Rennie Mackintosh, creating a warm, yet sophisticated lakeside retreat.
*Photograph by Karen Melvin*

**RIGHT**
A framed antique Tibetan prayer book sets the tone for the tranquil, Zen-like mood of this unique bath suite with twin showers.
*Photograph by Karen Melvin*

**FACING PAGE**
Asian-inspired fabrics used in a reversible bedding treatment complement an antique wall chest from China showcasing treasures from the Far East.
*Photograph by Karen Melvin*

It is that challenge to merge pleasing, functional environments with her clients' varied personalities that especially appeals to Lola. "I look at every job with fresh eyes," she says. "It's just like music: Every night you have a new audience, and they deserve your very best."

Putting clients' needs first has always been the foundation of Lola's business. "Certainly, clients are paying for my taste and expertise, but I want to help them realize their personalities and styles, not adapt to mine," she says. "If I can help them pay attention to the details of their lives, we'll be able to create environments that help them live fully and comfortably."

Lola's clients are found throughout the Midwest, and from California to New York to the Grand Cayman Islands. Articles about Lola and her work have been published in numerous national magazines, including various *Woman's Day* special interest magazines, as well as *Mpls. St. Paul Magazine, Midwest Home & Gardens,* Minneapolis *Star Tribune,* St. Paul *Pioneer Press* and *Window Fashions Design & Education Magazine.*

**TOP LEFT**
By replacing French doors that led to the pool with a large picture window, Lola improved traffic flow and reclaimed this living room for the adults in the family.
*Photograph by Karen Melvin*

**BOTTOM LEFT**
Lola used mahogany cabinetry and honed granite in this Wayzata kitchen and designed a room divider that keeps the living room view open while obscuring the kitchen.
*Photograph by Karen Melvin*

**FACING PAGE LEFT**
Modern appliances (dishwasher, beverage refrigerator and trash compactor) are neatly hidden behind reclaimed original cabinets in this 1919 Lake Minnetonka home's pantry.
*Photograph by Karen Melvin*

**FACING PAGE RIGHT**
The intricate ceiling painting and sumptuous bed treatment recreates the Queen Anne flavor of the historic Kellogg Mansion on Crocus Hill.
*Photograph by Karen Melvin*

# Q&A

## MORE ABOUT LOLA ...

NAME ONE THING MOST PEOPLE DON'T KNOW ABOUT YOU.

I'm an open book, so most people know that I was, and still am, an opera singer. They may not know, though, that I have performed at Carnegie Hall, recorded in Europe and appeared in the 1990 Academy Award-winning documentary, *In the Shadow of the Stars*.

DESCRIBE YOUR DESIGN PREFERENCES.

Classic design is what drives me, whether that design is French Country, Arts & Crafts or Bauhaus. The elements of good design are always present, no matter the form it takes. Really, it's the same as it is with classical music, which takes many forms, from Renaissance to Minimalism.

WHAT COLOR BEST DESCRIBES YOU AND WHY?

Red. It's vibrant, passionate, alive, energizing, energy-infused, committed, daring, dramatic—the color of life itself.

WHAT IS THE BEST PART OF BEING AN INTERIOR DESIGNER?

Enriching people's environments and lives, the new people you bring into your circle of friends and acquaintances, being able to learn and discover constantly. For me, being a designer is a positive experience.

LOLA WATSON INTERIOR DESIGN, LLC
Lola Watson, Allied Member ASID
275 Market Street, Suite 564
Minneapolis, MN 55405
612.604.1661
Fax 612.604.1662
www.lolawatson.com

# DEBORAH WEGENER

## DEBORAH·WEGENER INTERIORS, INC.

Every client has a dream of the perfect home. Some can eloquently communicate their desires while others are completely tongue-tied, as if trying to speak a foreign language for the first time. Nationally recognized interior designer Deborah Beal Wegener, ASID is gifted at translating this language from vision to inspired reality. Great design evokes emotion. Passionate in her philosophy that clients yearn for spaces that inspire emotional experiences, her aesthetic is one of inspired living. She imagines clients tucked into a corner beside a fireplace sipping tea on a winter afternoon or a mother and child snuggled into a window seat watching a flock of geese fly south. She gathers inspiration from geographic location, architecture, light and most importantly the desires and loves of her clients. In this way, she creates exceptionally original and striking interiors.

Wegener never repeats her designs in a cookie-cutter style. Taking influence from Classicism and Modernism, and staying abreast of trends, she is adeptly ambidextrous in creating breathtaking design. She fluently speaks a language of space, proportion, texture and color. With 25 years of design expertise, she is amazingly approachable and believes in a strong working collaboration with her clients.

A devoted clientele return time and time again with each successive home, as well as second and third homes across the United States. Her philosophy of juxtaposing great design with the belief that the best interiors "live well" has endeared Deborah to the next generation as they marry and create families of their own.

**ABOVE**
Friends delight in sharing a warm cup of tea in this antique-filled living room. The owner's extensive Staffordshire collection and hotel silver complement the George III caned settee.
*Photograph by Di Lewis*

**FACING PAGE**
With no detail overlooked, this bedroom entices guests with comfortable luxury. The mid-19th-century teak secretary combined with the crisp Brunschwig & Fils chintz creates a romantic retreat.
*Photograph by Di Lewis*

Keeping her firm small because Deborah prefers to have an active hand on each project, she works on approximately six projects a year. Her portfolio encompasses the highest-end residential homes to contemporary lofts to intimate, rustic lake cottages. Her uncompromising ability to ensure that spaces "work" has created professional spaces ranging from Wall Street offices to a 24-horse barn.

With this level of individuality one wonders if there is a constant in all of Wegener's projects. Indeed, each interior elicits an outpouring of emotion from her clients so that the completed project is a true reflection of them.

**TOP RIGHT**
The renovated kitchen provides a sleek modern update to a suburban townhome. Contrasting elements enable the kitchen to become an architectural focal point—glass mosaic tiles accompany anigre wood cabinets and concrete countertops.
*Photograph by Alex Steinberg*

**BOTTOM RIGHT**
This lakeside porch was furnished using a creative approach. When the scale of swings proved difficult, one was constructed using a teak garden settee. The antique carpenter's bench became a unique setting surface.
*Photograph by Deborah Wegener, ASID*

**FACING PAGE**
Antique furniture from CW Smith, Inc. creates an understated elegance in this breakfast room. The British Colonial rosewood table is wonderfully faded with a strong apron and base. The aged Calcutta marble tabletop is classic and practical for dining.
*Photograph by Di Lewis*

DEBORAH WEGENER INTERIORS, INC.
Deborah Beal Wegener, ASID
19550 Muirfield Circle
Shorewood, MN 55331
952.470.0948
Fax 952.470.1157

# PUBLISHING TEAM

DESIGNER MARTHA O'HARA INTERIORS, page 139

Brian G. Carabet, Publisher

John A. Shand, Publisher

Steve Darocy, Executive Publisher

Joanie Fitzgibbons, Associate Publisher

Beth Benton, Director of Design & Development

Julia Hoover, Director of Book Marketing & Distribution

Michele Cunningham-Scott, Art Director

Mary Elizabeth Acree, Graphic Designer

Emily Kattan, Graphic Designer

Ben Quintanilla, Graphic Designer

Elizabeth Gionta, Managing Editor

Rosalie Wilson, Editor

Lauren Castelli, Editor

Anita Kasmar, Editor

Kristy Randall, Senior Production Coordinator

Laura Greenwood, Production Coordinator

Jennifer Lenhart, Production Coordinator

Jessica Garrison, Traffic Coordinator

Carol Kendall, Project Manager

Beverly Smith, Project Manager

PANACHE PARTNERS, LLC

CORPORATE OFFICE

13747 Montfort Drive

Suite 100

Dallas, TX 75240

972.661.9884

www.panache.com

MINNESOTA OFFICE

612.423.1777

# THE PANACHE COLLECTION

### *Dream Homes* Series

Dream Homes of Texas
Dream Homes South Florida
Dream Homes Colorado
Dream Homes Metro New York
Dream Homes Greater Philadelphia
Dream Homes New Jersey
Dream Homes Florida
Dream Homes Southwest
Dream Homes Northern California
Dream Homes the Carolinas
Dream Homes Georgia
Dream Homes Chicago
Dream Homes California Southcoast
Dream Homes Washington, D.C.
Dream Homes the Western Deserts
Dream Homes Pacific Northwest
Dream Homes Minnesota
Dream Homes Ohio & Western Pennsylvania
Dream Homes California Central Coast
Dream Homes Connecticut
Dream Homes Los Angeles
Dream Homes Michigan
Dream Homes Tennessee
Dream Homes Greater Boston

### Additional Titles

Spectacular Hotels
Spectacular Golf of Texas
Spectacular Golf of Colorado
Spectacular Restaurants of Texas
Elite Portfolios
Spectacular Wineries of Napa Valley

### *City by Design* Series

City by Design Dallas
City by Design Atlanta
City by Design San Francisco Bay Area
City by Design Pittsburgh
City by Design Chicago
City by Design Charlotte
City by Design Phoenix, Tucson & Albuquerque
City by Design Denver

### *Perspectives on Design* Series

Perspectives on Design Florida

### *Spectacular Homes* Series

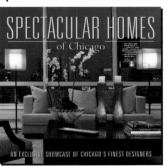

Spectacular Homes of Texas
Spectacular Homes of Georgia
Spectacular Homes of South Florida
Spectacular Homes of Tennessee
Spectacular Homes of the Pacific Northwest
Spectacular Homes of Greater Philadelphia
Spectacular Homes of the Southwest
Spectacular Homes of Colorado
Spectacular Homes of the Carolinas
Spectacular Homes of Florida
Spectacular Homes of California
Spectacular Homes of Michigan
Spectacular Homes of the Heartland
Spectacular Homes of Chicago
Spectacular Homes of Washington, D.C.
Spectacular Homes of Ohio
Spectacular Homes of Minnesota
Spectacular Homes of New England
Spectacular Homes of New York

**Visit www.panache.com or call
972.661.9884**

**PANACHE**
PANACHE PARTNERS, LLC

Creators of Spectacular Publications for
Discerning Readers

# Index of Designers

**DESIGNER** GUNKELMANFLESHER INTERIOR DESIGN, page 65